About the Author

Beverley Clack is Professor in Philosophy of Religion at Oxford Brookes University, UK. She is the author of *Sex and Death: A Reappraisal of Human Mortality.*

Freud on the Couch

A Critical Introduction to the Father of Psychoanalysis

Beverley Clack

ONEWORLD

A Oneworld Book

Published by Oneworld Publications 2013

Copyright © Beverley Clack 2013

ISBN 978-1-78074-262-5
eISBN 978-1-78074-263-2

Typeset by Cenveo Publishing Services
Printed and bound in Great Britain by
TJ International Ltd, Padstow, Cornwall, UK

Oneworld Publications
10 Bloomsbury Street
London WC1B 3SR
England
www.oneworld-publications.com

Stay up to date with the latest books,
special offers, and exclusive content from
Oneworld with our monthly newsletter

Sign up on our website
www.oneworld-publications.com

Contents

1
Freud's life and work

Sigmund Freud's ideas are familiar even if we have never read anything he has written. Most of us will have heard of the ego, the id, and the superego. When speaking of the actions and attitudes of others, we may use these terms for the conscious self, the unconscious that affects behaviour, and the internalized voice of societal norms. When someone makes a slip of the tongue and reveals what they really feel or think, we may well accuse them of making a 'Freudian slip'. If someone is overly concerned with order and keeping things tidy we may call them 'anal'. And if we suspect that one of our friends is ill at ease with their sexuality, we may find ourselves describing them as 'repressed'. These commonplaces go directly back to the work of Freud, drawing on key categories that shape his theory for understanding human behaviour: psychoanalysis.

Yet despite the way in which his language informs everyday conversation, few of us are likely to have read his books and fewer still will have read all of them. Most of us come to be aware of his ideas through popular culture. This might be in classic thrillers like Alfred Hitchcock's *Marnie* (1964), a film that uses psychoanalytic categories to trace a young woman's fear of sex to childhood abuse. Or in an altogether lighter vein, we might be introduced to Freud through the films of Woody Allen. Allen makes frequent, comic references in his films to the theories and practices of psychoanalysis. The best example of this is probably *Annie Hall* (1977), in which Allen explores the on–off relationship between comedian Alvy Singer and nightclub singer Annie. Much of the humour is drawn from relating Freud's ideas to the lives of these characters. At one point, Alvy describes Annie as 'polymorphously perverse', applying Freud's description of the child's ability to find pleasure in any part of the body: 'if I stroke your teeth or your kneecaps, you get excited'. Later, Alvy describes how he would have killed himself 'but I was in analysis with a strict Freudian and if you kill yourself they make you pay for the sessions you miss'. As this form of psychotherapy can involve meeting with an analyst five times a week, you get some sense of how expensive this would be!

Freud's image is immediately recognizable: a man in late middle age, grey-haired, bearded, with a steely gaze, self-possessed, wearing a heavy woollen three-piece suit, holding a cigar. Such is his fame that a range of tasteful (and sometimes tacky) memorabilia reflects this image, while at the same time enshrining our idea of who he is. There are numerous Freud dolls, all wearing neat and sombre suits, all bearded, all replicating that penetrating look. My favourite is a cuddly Freud that plays the Barbra Streisand song, 'The Way We Were'. This is an apt choice of tune for Freud; the line 'what's too painful to remember, we simply choose to forget' mirrors Freud's claim that the mind forces painful feelings and experiences from consciousness. Freud has even been turned into a plastic action figure, his 'special power' apparently lying in the cigar that he holds.

Freud is such a well-known figure, his image so iconic, that writing an introduction to his ideas is somewhat difficult. We may well think that we know what Freud has to say, whether or not we've actually read his books. Even if we have read them, our impression of what he says may have been gleaned from one or two of his major works: we might have read *The Three Essays on Sexuality*, *The Future of an Illusion*, or *The Interpretation of Dreams*. The problem with reading Freud in this way is that it can lead us to think of Freud as someone who is reducible to a few key ideas.

At the start of this book it is worth putting aside any pre-existing ideas about Freud so that a rather different, rather more complicated Freud can emerge. This Freud, I shall argue, has the power to speak to us, our world, and our concerns. To discover this Freud, we must consider some of his less familiar claims as well as those ideas that we may well have already encountered.

Freud wrote extensively: his books and articles fill some twenty-three volumes. Yet rediscovering Freud involves more than simply considering a greater number of these texts. It also involves paying attention to Freud's method as he goes about his endeavour to understand what it is to be human. This is a project that is not just about theoretical understanding but is also concerned with establishing methods for ameliorating the suffering that arises from human experience.

Freud is first and foremost a medical practitioner, who sought to cure those suffering from various forms of mental illness. His theories emerge from his practice. Moreover, these theories emerge at – and are shaped by – a particular point in history. At the end of the nineteenth century, psychology and the investigation of the brain are in their infancy. As such, he has no option but to attempt – tentatively – to create a vocabulary for the phenomena he is encountering.

This attempt to describe the processes behind mental illness is in itself a considerable undertaking. But this is not all that Freud does. He also relates his investigations of mental illness to a more general account of mental processes. Neither of these activities is easy; what makes reading Freud exciting are the places where we encounter the Freud who is not certain about his conclusions, who wishes to play with ideas and see where they lead him. It is this Freud that we will encounter here; the Freud who makes it his business to grapple with the pleasures and pains of human existence. As a result, this Freud continues to have much to offer his twenty-first century readers.

Here's an example. Freud is often portrayed as overly concerned with sex and, as we shall see, he has much to say about that subject. But he is also concerned with death. One of his most controversial suggestions is that just as humans are shaped by the sex-drive that leads to the creation of new things, to growth and expansion, so there is a 'death-drive' that draws them towards destructive cycles of repetition, disintegration, and eventually the welcome simplicity of not-being. While Freud is fascinated by this possibility and keen to explore it, he is also critical of it, unsure as to its merit and whether it is possible to give good evidence for such a notion:

> It may be asked whether and how far I am convinced of the truth of the hypotheses that have been set out in this paper. My answer would be that I am not convinced myself and that I do not seek to persuade other people to believe in them. Or, more precisely, that I do not know how far I believe in them (Freud, 1920: 59).

Here is an altogether more human Freud than the one we might expect from those iconic images; a mature individual at the peak of his powers. Spanning a period of some forty years, his writings show us someone who may not be 'making it up as he goes along', someone who is drawing upon the ideas of others but ultimately trying to develop a completely new way of talking about what it is to be human. This openness to disagreement along the way is not, it should be said, the only stance that he takes. The history of the founding of psychoanalysis as a discipline is full of instances when Freud dismisses those who disagree with what he takes to be fundamental aspects of his theory. But the more-hesitant Freud of this passage suggests something of the pleasure of reading him: he invites us to engage with his thought processes, recognizing the limitations of some of the speculative claims that he makes. He asks us to accompany him on a journey into the human mind. If we are prepared to go with him, it can be both an illuminating and challenging adventure.

The seventy-fifth anniversary of his death, in 2014, offers an opportunity to revisit the man whose work we think we know.

If we approach Freud's work with fresh eyes, we can see, along-side his first readers, the innovation as well as the strangeness of his work. In a culture that is so familiar with 'Freudian' ideas, we have largely lost that sense of surprise. In attempting to regain it we might recover the controversial nature of his thought for an age that has rather lazily accepted his ideas with little sense of what Freud actually said.

We start to get some sense of the creativity of Freud's approach if we consider the way in which key developments in his thoughts emerge from the backdrop of his life. To adopt this approach is to bring to the fore Freud's starting point for reflection. The personal and the individual are placed firmly at the centre of his attempt to understand human life and culture. Ideas and values are not abstract; they do not drop ready-formed into the human world but emerge from the experience of the individual. This does not mean, as we shall see, that it is impossible to make general claims about what it is to be a human being: far from it. It simply requires us to think more deeply about the different experiences, processes, and events that have shaped the way in which we, as individuals, engage with our world. Considering Freud's life – and particularly his early life – allows us to grasp something of the personal struggles and concerns that influence the shape his practice and theory take. Just as he encouraged his patients to lie on a couch and tell him their stories, so there is no better way to proceed than by asking the same of Freud.

Freud's early life

Sigismund Schlomo Freud was born on 6 May 1856 in Freiberg in Moravia, the first son of Jacob and Amalia Freud. Amalia had seven more children but Sigi remained her favourite and most favoured child. Freud was viewed as something of a child prodigy by his doting mother, who did everything she could to cultivate a sense of her beloved boy as a fledgling intellectual. Family life was adapted to his needs: when the family's piano disturbed his studies, it was quickly removed.

Amalia, Jacob's third wife, was an attractive young woman some twenty years younger than her husband. Sigmund (the name he adopted, first at school and then, permanently, at university) was therefore born into an extended family with a complicated network of interrelated, cross-generational relationships. The children of Jacob's first marriage were considerably older than Sigmund. The eldest, Emanuel, was older than his stepmother, Amalia. One of Emanuel's sons – Sigmund's nephew, despite being a year older than his uncle – was Sigi's first little friend. Describing these overlapping relationships gives us a good sense of just how complicated was Freud's family life.

The lack of a clear distinction between the generations in Sigmund's first experiences of life no doubt contributed to his fascination with the peculiarities and complexities of human relationships. In later life, he recalled his sense of confusion about the identity of his younger sister Anna's father. Was Anna's father the elderly Jacob or Sigi's dashing half-brother Philipp?

Financial problems compelled the family to move, first to Leipzig and then, in 1860, to the Leopoldstadt, in Vienna. Here, Freud found himself at the heart of the Jewish ghetto. Vienna was an ambivalent city for Jews. Anti-Semitism was rife but, at the same time, liberal reforms meant that Jewish boys like Sigmund could dream of 'making it'. Freud recalled being told by a fortune teller that he would 'probably grow up to be a Cabinet Minister' (Freud, 1900: 193). Yet, living in the ghetto, he could not escape his awareness of being a Jewish boy in a society that, at best, looked on Jews with suspicion and, at worst, made sure that Jews firmly knew their place in the life of the city. The family was not religious but was still castigated for being Jewish, confronting Sigmund with the deep-rooted nature of such prejudices.

These prejudices had very personal consequences for the young Sigi. When Sigmund was twelve, his father told him a disturbing and dispiriting story that revealed his apparent acceptance of the limitations of being Jewish. Out walking, Jacob was confronted by a Gentile, who knocked his hat from his head and yelled at him to get off the pavement because he was a Jew. Sigmund was dismayed when he asked, 'what did you do?' and his father replied that he had, of course, picked up his hat. What alternative was there? (Freud, 1900: 197) Sigmund's hero at the time was the great military commander Hannibal. The contrast between his father's (apparent) cowardice and his hero's willingness to fight must have been disturbing, to say the least.

Jacob's lack of heroism may have been pragmatic but it had a lasting effect on Freud's sense of his father. It seems to have influenced the shape taken by the most controversial of his theories, the Oedipus complex. As we shall see in Chapter 3, when we consider the complex in depth, the Oedipus complex takes a variety of forms but at its heart is simply defined. Between the ages of three and five, each child experiences the desire dramatized in the story of the mythical Greek King Oedipus. Oedipus, an adopted child, inadvertently kills his father and marries his mother. Freud claims that in the phantasies of every child, there lies a similar desire: they wish to kill the parent of the same sex in order to have sex with the parent of the opposite sex.

Before we go much further we should consider what Freud means by that word 'phantasy', not only because it affects what Freud means when he claims that the child 'desires' these shocking outcomes but also because it becomes a key concept in the work of the psychoanalysts who followed him.

Jean Laplanche and Jean-Bertrand Pontalis point out that in German, '*phantasie*' refers to the world of the imagination, both in terms of 'its contents and the creative activity which animates it'. We may think of phantasy as less significant than reality but the psychoanalyst's intention is to show how phantasies have a powerful effect upon the way in which the 'real' world is perceived.

What does Freud mean when he claims the child has murderous and incestuous feelings? His focus is not on the 'real' relationship between parent and child but with the desires or wishes of the child. These are shaped by the child's ignorance of what sex and death actually involve. When the child thinks of sex with the parent, they wrap this up with the desire to possess totally the parent of the opposite sex. Likewise, when they think of the death of the parent of the same sex, their desire is for their absence, rather than the physical destruction of that parent. This does not mean that we should think of such imaginings as powerless or trivial: far from it. Such phantasies might be forgotten as we age but they leave their imprint on the kind of adult sexual relationships we have, as well as forming the bedrock for one's character.

When Freud refers to the Oedipus complex, he does so to establish his theory of sexuality. However, it is not simply a theory that emerges from his intellectual investigations; it also owes much to Freud's personal battles with and range of feelings towards his own father. If his young, glamorous mother, who clearly preferred Sigi to her other children, was his father's property, this fallible (dare one say cowardly?) father could be overcome. In adulthood, Sigmund felt that he had, indeed, surpassed the less-than-heroic Jacob. In his writings, there are intimations of this difficult relationship with his father that suggest something of the way in which his personal struggles influence the shape his theories take.

In *The Interpretation of Dreams*, Freud describes an embarrassing childhood experience in which he urinated in his parents' bedroom while they were present. Jacob's frustrated response to this annoying and messy intrusion was: 'the boy will come to nothing!' (Freud, 1900: 216). Not surprisingly, Freud wants to prove his father wrong. But the determination to challenge his father's ideas about him is not all that he derives from this experience. Rather than see his personal struggle with a less-than-sympathetic father as precisely that – personal – Freud moves from his own experience to consider the tensions between all children and their parents. As he conceives it, the parent–child relationship is never straightforward. Our relationships with our parents are always ambivalent, for the parent is both loved and hated. If Freud hadn't loved his father as well as despised him, he may have found it easier to deal with his feelings. He could simply have rejected him.

These personal tensions affect the way in which Freud constructs his theory of the Oedipus complex. Freud's focus is invariably upon the relationship between the son and his father; the relationship between mother and daughter is less-explicitly addressed. Undoubtedly this reflects his less troubled relationship with his mother. She is adored; she adores him: what more is there to say? But such personal struggles are not without impact, for they go on to shape the theory that Freud formulates. Feminist commentators like Christiane Olivier and Angela Carter suggest that this leads to a weakness in his theory, for he fails to deal adequately with the role the mother plays. Emphasising the paternal at the expense of the maternal leads him to focus on male rather than female experiences and relationships. It takes the theories of the later psychoanalyst Melanie Klein and her reflections on the importance of the mother, in the 1940s, to redress the balance.

The ambivalence felt by the son towards the father is further personalized in an incident that takes placing during Freud's first visit to Athens. Seeing the Acropolis for the first time, Freud is overcome with emotion. Analysing this emotion, he discovers that it is guilt. Why guilt? Because when he sees the Acropolis, he not only sees an ancient building, he understands the significance of this place for western culture. It is the place where the roots of western democracy, philosophy, and art were established. His ill-educated father would not have made this connection but his better-educated, more cultured son can. Here is the source of Freud's guilt: he has surpassed his father by being better-educated and more cultured. But feeling that sense of victory does not simply bring pleasure: it also reminds him that the all-powerful image of his father – his first hero – has been lost, and lost because of Freud's own actions (Freud, 1936). A painful truth about the nature of life has been grasped. Life is never just about growth and development; it also involves disillusion and loss.

Doctor Freud

A precocious, bookish childhood, pampered as his mother's favourite, was followed in 1873 by medical studies at the University of Vienna. Taught by the noted physiologist Ernst Brücke (1819–92) and the scientist Hermann von Helmholtz (1821–94), Freud wanted to be a research scientist, rather than a medical practitioner. His plans were disrupted when he fell in love with Martha Bernays. Wanting to marry (they did so in 1886) and recognizing that being Jewish would make advancement difficult, because of the prejudices of his day, he had to think pragmatically about a career that could finance the marital home. This meant pursuing a medical career with paying clients rather than the hand-to-mouth existence of the scientific researcher. However, Freud was to establish no ordinary medical practice. His interest lay in treating mental diseases and he particularly wanted to explore the roots of the most discussed mental illness of his day: hysteria.

Hysteria is a troubling and troublesome diagnosis with which to engage. Today, it has largely disappeared as a medical diagnosis; its symptoms have been subsumed into a number of different mental conditions and disorders. In Freud's day, hysteria was identified according to a range of symptoms whose origins could not be traced to any physical ailment. The sufferer might exhibit feelings of suffocation, nervous coughing, dramatic fits, paralysis of the limbs, fainting spells, an inability to speak, loss of hearing, forgetting their own language, speaking in an unfamiliar language, vomiting, and an inability to eat or drink. The hysteric cut a disturbing figure, as we can see from photographs collected by one of the main investigators in Freud's time, Jean-Martin Charcot (see Figure 1).

Most sufferers were female but Freud courted controversy by arguing that men, too, could be hysterics. In Charcot's photographs we see women 'out of control', caught up in a private reverie. These images are deeply disturbing and we may feel uncomfortable looking at their intimate depictions. The women's contorted bodies suggest that they are caught up in a private passion; it is difficult not to feel like a peeping Tom as we look at them. Depictions of the out-of-control hysteric both fascinate and repel us, leaving us feeling deeply uneasy.

Freud's method for treating such women came from his collaborations with other medical practitioners. (It also, as we shall see in Chapter 2, emerged from the relationships he forged with the hysterics who attended his practice.) Early influences from the medical profession were Theodor Meynert (1833–92), director of a psychiatric clinic in Vienna and Jean-Martin Charcot (1825–93), director of the Salpêtrière asylum in Paris. Charcot's influence on Freud's approach extended beyond his attempt to disclose the story that lay at the heart of the hysteric's suffering; Freud was attracted to and sought to emulate Charcot's writing style, which drew upon an eclectic range of sources and literary devices.

Working alongside people such as Charcot enabled Freud to develop his approach to conditions such as hysteria. He became less concerned with establishing the biological causes of such disturbances and more with finding psychological explanations. Working with another doctor, Josef Breuer (1842–1925), enabled him to move more directly into the investigation of what caused hysteria. He began to develop theories of mental illness that took

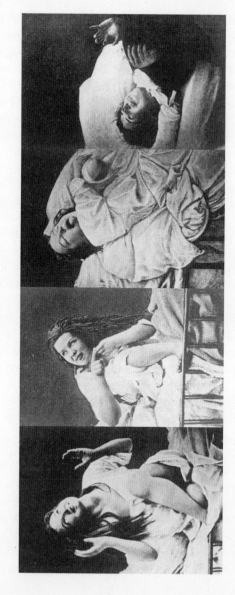

Figure 1 Images of hysterics at Salpêtrière (Credit: Wikimedia images)

into account the role sexuality played in forming the symptoms of such illnesses. In 1886, drawing upon these training experiences, he opened his own private practice to treat people suffering from various forms of neuropathology (or mental illness).

Freud's experience of working with Breuer and the hysterics they sought to cure led him to formulate a new understanding of the mind. In investigating hysteria, he and Breuer concluded that the illnesses they were attempting to treat resulted from feelings and ideas that had been suppressed; driven from consciousness. A common view of hysteria at the time was that it arose from the degeneracy of the hysteric. If we look again at Charcot's photographs, the apparently sexual nature of their reveries was taken as evidence that these were immoral, promiscuous women, whose illnesses revealed their true nature. Freud's investigations suggested a radically different view: the hysteric was not an evil degenerate. Instead, he argued that at the root of the hysteric's illness was 'an unacceptable idea' accompanying a traumatic event, often sexual. Rather than accept this idea, the hysteric was, in fact, too moral and as a result sought to detach herself from it entirely.

A good example is found in the brief association Freud had with Katharina, a rather sulky eighteen-year-old inn-keeper's daughter, whom he met while on holiday (Breuer and Freud, 1893–5: 125–34). In conversation, Katharina tells him that for the last two years she has suffered from recurring anxiety attacks of being suffocated, accompanied by hallucinations of an unknown face. Freud traces these symptoms to abuse at the hands of her father (although in the case study he names Katharina's uncle as the abuser: a sign of the surprising queasiness he sometimes displays when addressing the disturbing world of sexual desire). The symptoms arise after Katharina witnesses a shocking event. Searching for her cousin, she has found her in bed with her father. Shocked, her mind goes blank; she feels dizzy and disorientated. She takes to her bed. Eventually, she tells her mother what she has witnessed; as a result, her mother leaves her father.

Katharina's anxiety could be linked to the trauma of a family break-up but would that account for the disturbing visions of the unknown face? Freud goes deeper and uncovers a memory of an attempted seduction by her father, when Katharina was fourteen. A mere child, she had not understood what he was trying to do as sexual. This knowledge only arises when she sees her father with her cousin. The scene is accompanied by what becomes the unacceptable thought: 'now he's doing with her what he wanted to do with me that night and those other times' (Breuer and Freud, 1893–5: 131).

Initially, she resists this thought, which she finds disgusting, and drives it from her mind. In Freud's terms, she 'represses' it. The notion of repression forms a key part of Freud's theory: here it is understood as the process by which unacceptable thoughts are driven from consciousness. Unable to acknowledge her experience, Katharina – and the hysteric more generally – falls prey to symptoms which play out that which is not acknowledged, dramatically, on the body. When she is pressed, it becomes clear that the face she keeps seeing is her father's, enraged that her revelations have cost him his marriage. What might have become a pain in her mind (if you like, an emotional wound) becomes instead a pain in her body, because she has attempted to drive all thought of it from her mind. Freud's argument is that the psychic energy generated by the emotion has to go somewhere. In Katharina's case, it has been transformed into anxiety attacks accompanied by hallucinations that, when analysed, reveal a sad story of attempted abuse and betrayal.

Realizing the power of such repressed feelings to create the physical symptoms associated with hysteria leads Freud to develop a method for seeking to bring what is unconscious into consciousness. This involves a technique that necessitates talking through what is troubling the patient. One of Breuer's patients, known as 'Anna O', likened the process to 'chimney-sweeping'.

This method of cleaning out the mind involved 'free-associating': saying whatever came into one's mind, however ridiculous, apparently meaningless or shameful. By analysing the connections made by the patient it becomes possible to trace the symptoms from which they are suffering back to their source. This 'cathartic' method becomes the basis for Freud's postulation of 'psycho-analysis' as a way of dealing with mental disturbances. Once the roots of the symptom are identified, the symptom disappears. 'Analysing the psyche' (or the mind) enables what is unconscious to be made conscious, giving the patient the possibility of a life once more held in their own hands.

Importantly, Freud makes the jump from these reflections as a way of explaining hysteria to applying them, more generally, to an account of what it is to be a human being. The hysteric was not conscious of her repressed feelings and desires. But just because such feelings were no longer conscious – were, instead, unconscious – did not mean that they were unable to affect her life. Far from it: they had devastating consequences for her ability to live in the world. Rather than limit the significance of the unconscious for explaining mental illness, Freud goes on to apply it more generally to all human beings.

Western attempts to theorize the self have tended to draw attention to the idea that human individuals are best defined through those elements of the self which are conscious and reflective. I am a reflective, conscious person who knows who I am, what I believe, and what I want to do. The idea of the unconscious challenges such views. What Freud concludes from his work with hysterics is that there is an agency within the self of which we know little, an agency that is unconscious but which has the power to affect our actions. In the experience of the hysteric, we have but an extreme case. Individuals are more complex than we might like to think.

In *The Psychopathology of Everyday Life* (1901), Freud provides examples of the power of the unconscious when he outlines examples of apparently trivial actions – forgetting, slips of the tongue, jokes, losing things – that, when analysed, reveal much about which the individual is neither aware nor conscious. In a personal example, I was going through a difficult period with a relative when I lost a ring that she had given me. At the time, I thought nothing of it, writing it off as merely an irritation. Reading the *Psychopathology* many years later suggested a different interpretation: far from being 'an accident', my loss of her gift revealed an unconscious desire to be rid of her. I couldn't lose her but I could lose her ring!

By bringing together the experiences of the hysteric and our own actions, Freud intends to reveal the extent to which all are driven by unconscious desires as well as the rational motives of which we are aware. Explaining this idea, Freud liked to use the model of an iceberg. Rationality and the conscious self form the part of the iceberg of the human mind that is above the surface but the vast majority lies beneath the waves, unknown, unexplored, waiting to be discovered.

Overcoming the Father: self-analysis and the development of psychoanalysis

Freud's work with hysterics enabled the notion of the unconscious to come to the fore. His self-analysis following the death of his father in 1896 furthered this work as well as enabling his clinical practice to develop.

It is not surprising that his father's death should have sparked the need for deeper self-understanding. The death of a parent towards whom one has complex and contradictory emotions is often more difficult to cope with than that of a parent towards whom one has a clear set of feelings. It challenges not only who we think they were but also who we think we are. Coming as it did in Freud's fortieth year, his father's death coincided with his entry into middle age: a time when it is customary to review one's life.

Freud's relationship with his mother seems relatively straightforward. She was and always would be the much-loved mother who believed in him. In contrast, Jacob's death affected Freud deeply and proved to be the catalyst not only for deeper self-examination but also for the method that led to his new understanding of the self and, ultimately, to a new school of thought.

Crucial to this self-analysis was the investigation and interpretation of his dreams. We are often dismissive of dreams, seeing them as meaningless detritus derived from the events of the day. Freud argued that if one was prepared to spend time analysing dreams, through the same process of free association used with his hysterical patients, it was possible to understand them quite differently.

Far from being meaningless, dreams offer a way into the world of the unconscious. Interpreting dream material takes time, not least because the meaning of a dream is not obvious. In dreams, unconscious wishes are disguised to escape the censorship of the conscious self that repressed such unacceptable ideas and feelings in the first place. Through dream analysis it is possible to come to greater self-knowledge, uncovering what is going on beneath the surface consciousness of day-to-day concerns and of discovering the stranger within. (We will return to the importance of dreams to Freud's theory in Chapter 4.)

In 1900, Freud's work came to fruition. He published *The Interpretation of Dreams*, a book that emerged from the rigours of his self-analysis and set the scene for the development of the psychoanalytic movement. Key ideas were emerging: not least, the importance of childhood sexuality and the desires and fears of the Oedipus complex.

From his work on hysteria and his dream analysis, Freud came to believe that sexuality is vital for understanding human beings.

In works such as *Three Essays on Sexuality* (1905) and *On the Sexual Theories of Children* (1908), he offers an expanded view of what sexuality involves. When we talk of 'sex' we tend to assume that we are talking about intimate physical acts and, particularly, of acts which relate to reproduction. Freud broadens this out, suggesting that in the human sexual realm things are more complicated. The sexual aim or 'drive' is not always directed to the same end; it is not always concerned with mating to ensure reproduction and the continuation of the species. Different objects can become the focus for the drive. For some, a partner of the same sex will be the object for the drive; for others, in forms of fetishism, a pair of shoes. The aim and the object are not 'soldered together'; they can be separated. This means that if we are to understand human sexuality, we must focus not only on sexual activity but also people's imaginings about sex. Human sexuality is not purely about the animal drive to reproduce; the form it takes for any individual is constructed and shaped by the imagination.

Understanding sexuality in this more complicated way leads to another controversial aspect of Freud's theory: the idea of infantile sexuality. Freud argues that sex does not simply arrive ready-made in the child's world alongside adolescence and puberty. The infant, too, is a sexual being. But the infant's sexuality should not be read as we might adult sexuality: that is, with the view that their focus is with the genitals and with achieving sexual intercourse. Sexuality passes through a series of stages: the oral stage (when the pleasures of sucking dominate), the anal stage (when the pleasures of bowel control dominate) and the phallic stage (when the pleasures of masturbation are discovered) (Freud, 1905b: 173–91). As the child passes through these stages, different imaginings or 'phantasies' come to shape what he or she finds pleasurable.

Sex is shaped, then, by the imagination. As the child experiences the different pleasures of the body, it is also seeking to understand the world, and particularly what mum and dad do together when the child is not present. Children develop sexual theories about the nature of sex based on the limited evidence available – bloody sheets or knickers, strange cries from their parents' room. These theories may later be displaced and corrected but the imaginings that greet such experiences continue to exert a powerful – if unconscious – effect on how the adults' sexuality is constructed. The sexual realm rather than being something obvious, becomes in Freud's theory a place of mystery, which must be explored.

From 1902 Freud's views began to attract attention and followers. In 1908 there was sufficient interest to hold the First International Conference of the Psychoanalytical Movement, in Salzburg. Freud had moved from being a lone practitioner engaging with neurotic illness while conducting an investigation of his own life and experiences, to working with others who were equally committed to exploring the importance of the unconscious for human self-understanding.

It is not altogether surprising that his ideas should have proved popular with the intellectuals of his day. Despite their often controversial and challenging form, the idea of the unconscious was far from alien in the German-speaking world of his day. Of particular significance for these developing ideas were the philosophies of Arthur Schopenhauer (1788–1860) and Friedrich Nietzsche (1844–1900). Both formulated accounts of the forces that lay beneath the surface of consciousness. For Schopenhauer, the mind was best understood as 'a sheet of water of some depth … the distinctly conscious ideas are merely surface'; an image that immediately resonates with Freud's analogy of the iceberg. Similarly, Nietzsche uses '*das Es*' – the It – to describe the impersonal and unconscious forces that have the power to shape our actions. Eventually, Freud adopted Nietzsche's language as his label for the unconscious.

Despite these similarities – and indeed borrowings – Freud went out of his way to deny his familiarity with the ideas of these two philosophers. He claimed that he had only come to Schopenhauer's ideas 'late in life' (Freud, 1925a: 29) and that 'he did not know' Nietzsche's.

Why the desire to separate his ideas from those that have gone before? Freud was extremely well read and it is difficult to believe that he did not know of the similarities between his ideas and those of Schopenhauer and Nietzsche. Followers such as Paul Federn and Arnold Zweig are on record as pointing out to Freud where some of these connections lie. There seems something rather strange about Freud's desire to distance himself from other thinkers. Pointing to theorists who suggest similar conclusions would seem to help establish the truth of his claims.

A personal reason can be identified behind this stance. Returning to that embarrassing vignette of the little Sigmund urinating in his parents' bedroom, we remember his father's frustrated response: 'the boy will come to nothing!' How powerful the desire to prove the father wrong! How better to do this than to be the 'father' of a new science that has the power to revolutionize the way humanity is understood? (If we are tempted to read such a claim as a judgement on Freud's character, we might want to consider the extent to which our own lives have been shaped by different responses to our parents. Do we follow their lead or prove them wrong in their judgements about life or, indeed, about ourselves and our failings?) If we accept this context, the desire to affirm his status as progenitor of an innovative system of thought is entirely understandable.

The history of those early years of the psychoanalytic movement suggests something of the strength and (on several occasions) disruptive power of Freud's relationships with men and women. Perhaps surprisingly, given Freud's reputation as a patriarch who claimed that 'biology is destiny', his difficult relationships tended to be with men, while his relationships with women were invariably warm, supportive, and long-lasting. But if we see him as concerned to establish a new way of thinking that will displace his father's negative assessment of him, his difficult relationships with rival male colleagues start to make more sense.

A couple of examples will provide an indication of the complexity and depth of Freud's relationships. Carl Gustav Jung (1875–1961) was in many ways his greatest collaborator, until a spectacular falling-out that split the psychoanalytic movement. The son of a Swiss pastor, Jung studied medicine and worked at the renowned psychiatric clinic at Burghölzli. Impressed by Freud's work on dreams and hysteria, Jung became a supporter of his ideas and began to correspond with Freud in 1906. Their correspondence was intense and warm but very much cast Freud in the role of mentor and Jung as his pupil. Despite – or even because of – this, Freud, to the irritation of others in the psychoanalytic movement, was quick to award Jung the role of heir apparent. But there was nothing cosy about this master/pupil relationship. From the beginning there were differences in their respective approaches to sexuality: Jung refused to accept Freud's all-pervasive account, seeking to understand the main force in human life as a more generalized mental energy. He was also open to a more mystical and religious approach to life: attitudes that Freud would dismiss (as we shall see in Chapter 5) as mere illusion.

Eventually, the stresses and strains of a relationship between two powerful personalities and intellects proved too much. Jung's bitterness at being painted as the young apprentice came to the fore and resentment at what he perceived as Freud's dogmatism led to a final break.

As Peter Gay notes, this break began with 'a trivial incident'. In 1912, Jung took umbrage when Freud failed to visit him during a trip to see Ludwig Binswanger, who was thought to be terminally ill. Freud's response to Jung's irritated enquiry as to why they had not met did not mention Binswanger's illness. This reflected Binswanger's wish that no one should know he was ill. However, it also suggests that Freud was getting a little tired of Jung's emotional outbursts and demands on his time and that he had no intention of smoothing things over with his erstwhile disciple. If the break was not yet open, a mental division had opened between them. On a lecture tour to the United States later that year, Jung explicitly rejected Freud's theories of childhood sexuality, the Oedipus complex, and the role of sexuality in the formation of neurotic illness. Eventually, in 1914, Jung resigned as President of the International Psychoanalytic Association after a year or more of public wrangling and fighting.

The pattern of his relationship with Jung was not unfamiliar to Freud. Idolization (on both sides), friction, falling out; this was a pattern that could be seen in his relationships with other men, including the physician Wilhelm Fliess (1858–1928) and the analyst Alfred Adler (1870–1937).

More lasting, stable relationships were to be had with women, for whom the psychoanalytic movement provided a flourishing context. If psychoanalysis was initially characterized as 'the Jewish Science' because of the number of Jewish thinkers and practitioners, it could equally well be described as 'the women's science'. Its early ideas were shaped by women analysts, such as Hermine Hug-Hellmuth (1871–1924), Helene Deutsch (1884–1982), Karen Horney (1885–1952), Ruth Mack Brunswick (1897–1946), and Joan Riviere (1883–1962). The development of psychoanalysis after Freud's death was shaped by the colossal figures of Melanie Klein (1882–1960) and Freud's daughter Anna Freud (1895–1982). Analysts such as Hanna Segal, Rosine Perelberg, Julia Kristeva, and Jessica Benjamin continue to shape its contemporary theory and practice. Given the attraction of psychoanalysis for women, it is perhaps not so very surprising that Freud developed a number of intellectual friendships with women. Princess Marie Bonaparte (1882–1962), who helped fund the Freuds' escape from Nazi Germany, was a close confidante as well as a lively conversation partner. But perhaps the most interesting of these female friends is Lou Andreas-Salomé (1861–1937).

Russian and from a wealthy aristocratic background, Lou appears as a woman born out of her time, displaying qualities that we might more readily associate with our own age. Arriving in Vienna in the midst of the Freud–Jung battles of 1912, Lou had a reputation as a 'free-thinker', cutting, in many ways, a somewhat scandalous figure. This reputation was based upon her part, when she was a young woman, in a bizarre triangular relationship with Nietzsche and the philosopher and writer Paul Rée. While Lou cast this arrangement in intellectual terms, the men fell in love with her; the experiment in alternative living failed spectacularly, torn apart by jealousy and misunderstanding. As a somewhat older woman, she quickly established herself as an important member of the psychoanalytic community, bringing, as she put it, 'the invisible figure' of Nietzsche into Freud's inner circle. Interested in expanding understandings of female sexuality, Lou refused to see her womanhood as a negative and believed that 'the feminine in its essence partakes of a "primordial fusion with the All in which we repose"'. Woman is 'at home' in the processes of the natural world in a way in which man is not. (Chapter 5 considers the centrality of the claim that we are not at home in the world for Freud's account of religion.) Woman is, for Andreas-Salomé, 'the fortunate animal', blessed with an equilibrium not possessed by the restless male.

Over the years, Freud came to rely increasingly on Lou, respecting her intelligence and valuing their correspondence, which ran to over two hundred letters. Lou also provided invaluable support for Freud's daughter Anna, who was to be an eminent psychoanalyst in her own right. Anna had a fraught relationship with her mother, Martha; Lou seems to have taken on the role of adoptive mother. Freud and Lou referred to Anna as their 'Daughter Anna', a designation which suggests something of their intimacy. This is not to say that there were no theoretical disputes between Freud and Andreas-Salomé. Yet in contrast to Freud's problematic relationship with Jung, these differences could be discussed without fear of their friendship breaking down. Was there less at stake psychologically in a relationship with a woman? Was there less of a power struggle with someone of the opposite sex? Given Freud's relationship with his father and the shadow that cast over his sense of self and his need for achievement, relationships with women may have been less emotionally overlaid than relationships with rival males.

War and death

Alongside such intellectual tussles and companionship, world events played their part in defining Freud's views. The catastrophe of the Great War of 1914–18 had a considerable impact on the direction of his thinking, forcing him to engage directly with the problems of being an individual in society. While 'civilization' offers us many advantages – community, association, support against the forces of nature – it also necessitates suppressing the animal instincts that are part of our make-up. If we are to live in society we need to find ways of curbing the desires for sex and violence.

The Great War saw Freud having to amend aspects of his theory. Until then, his concerns had been with the sexual instincts. The question had been with how to understand the nature of sexuality. In particular, he had argued that humans were driven by the desire for maximizing pleasure and minimizing pain: what he called 'the pleasure-principle'. As we grow into maturity, the excesses of the desire for pleasure have to be held in check by the recognition of reality, particularly the way in which our desires must be curbed if we are to live together in society. In the wake of war, these reflections take a different turn. How are we to understand the sources of human aggression? In response, Freud speculates that another instinct resides alongside the sexual instinct. If the sexual instinct is connected with the drive to create new life and new things, the other instinct seeks a return to the tranquillity before animate life; it is a drive that encourages disintegration and death.

Freud's notion of the 'death-drive' is controversial, because it is unclear quite what evidence can be provided. In the context of a world that seems to be collapsing upon itself, it might make more sense. Against the backdrop of the horror of trench warfare, there seems some justification for Freud's damning conclusion that: 'the aim of all life is death' (Freud, 1920: 38). The question becomes how to respond to this terrifying knowledge.

The period following the crushing defeat of the Austro-German armies did little to allay the sense of a society that was collapsing. The economic upheaval that followed the imposition of reparations on Germany and her allies was felt by Freud as by countless others. It was difficult to find patients who were able to pay for analysis. He lost his savings and struggled to keep his practice afloat.

While the wider world was reeling from the horrors of war and its continuing ramifications, tragedy struck at the heart of his family. Freud's favourite daughter, his 'Sunday child' Sophie, died in the 1920 influenza epidemic. It was a terrible blow. 'I do not know whether cheerfulness will ever call on us again', he wrote to his friend Kata Levy. This loss was followed in 1923 by the death of Sophie's four-and-a-half-year-old son, Heinele. If anything, this was an even greater shock than Sophie's death. Freud believed that, for the first time in his life, he was suffering from depression. Life had lost any sense of meaning and he confided to his friend Otto Rie that '[Heinele] meant the future to me and thus has taken the future away with him'. In the same year, Freud underwent the first of many operations for the cancer of the jaw that was to leave him in agony for much of the time until his death in 1939. It was a sad and painful time.

Given such events, it is tempting to see Freud as the psychologist who reveals the misery of the human condition, not just in his theory but also his life. That would be a mistake. Alongside the all-too-common loss of loved ones, there is also the development of his strong working relationship with his youngest daughter, Anna. Famed for her development of child psychoanalysis, she also developed theories that emphasized the significance of the conscious, rational ego; theories that would foster and influence Freud's later account of the self.

In his early theory, Freud was concerned to map the workings of the unconscious. This entailed developing a model of the mind that sought to explain the way in which the conscious and unconscious worlds interact. To do this, Freud employed what has been called a 'topographical model'. This entailed thinking of the mind as an interconnected series of regions. There is the conscious mind, which is rational and self-aware. There is the unconscious, which contains the desires that have been driven from consciousness. There is also the pre-conscious mind, that part of the mind where unconscious desires and feelings start to make themselves open to consciousness in, for example, the world of dreams.

In the later theory – dating from 1923 – a different model emerges, which seeks to define the three 'structures' of the mind. He uses the terms 'ego', for the rational, conscious mind; 'id', for the unconscious mind; and 'superego', for the external world of parental and societal mores that has been internalized.

If the early theory was designed to map the workings of the unconscious (how does what is unconscious become conscious?), the later theory emphasizes the way analysis seeks to strengthen the ego so that it might withstand the pressures of the id. In this we see Anna's influence; her significance to Freud was immense. As he lay dying he told his doctor, Max Schur, 'Fate has been good to me, that it should still have granted me the relationship to such a woman – I mean Anna, of course.' This comment reflects a broader idea in his work. Human life is shaped by two needs: 'the compulsion to work, which was created by external necessity, and the power of love' (Freud, 1930: 101). His losses suggest that life cannot be defined simply by growth and pleasure; it also involves vulnerability and pain. The only way through is to find work that gives shape and stability to life, and to invest in one's relationships.

The emergence of the Nazis as a political force, from the turmoil of the post-war period, had a considerable impact on Freud's life. In 1933, his books were burnt along with those of other Jewish academics and thinkers. 'What progress we are making,' he noted wryly to Ernest Jones. 'In the Middle Ages they would have burnt me; nowadays they are content with burning my books.' The Nazis, of course, were not content to stop with burning books. Their 'Final Solution' touched his family in ways that, thankfully, he was never to know. His sister Adolfine starved to death in Theresienstadt, while his sisters Maria and Pauline were murdered, probably in Auschwitz, in 1942.

The annexing of Austria in 1938 made life in Vienna impossible for the Freud family. On the morning of 15 March, a group of *Sturm Abteilung* thugs raided his home but left when confronted by a furious Freud. His daughter Anna's arrest by the Gestapo (she was held for a day) was more disturbing. These events led friends to make preparations for the Freuds to find sanctuary in England. The family left Vienna for what was to become Freud's final home – 20 Maresfield Gardens in North London – in June 1938. Freud died in September the following year. Freud was in extreme pain from the cancer that had destroyed his jaw, and asked to be given a final, fatal dose of morphine.

Freud's life and legacy

What might we discern from this consideration of Freud's life and work? He may be developing ideas that fundamentally alter the way in which we think about human life but it is worth noting the way in which the details of his life are not remote from those of his readers. The struggles of Freud's life are not alien from our own. How are we to engage with complex family structures in an age when divorce is frequent and second families far from uncommon? How are we to balance the different demands that press upon us: career and family, friends and ambition? How are we to engage with the tragedies of everyday life: the loss of parents, children, and friends? At the same time, international events – impersonal and beyond individual control – have, in their turn, an impact upon the pattern of each life and the course that it takes.

In a culture that has become increasingly obsessed with the lives of celebrities, this is far from an insignificant point. We might not be famous; at times, our lives might seem mundane and dull. However, one thing unites us all: the need to grapple with similar issues and to find resolutions to the problems of living.

Freud offers us more than simply 'a life for our time', as the subtitle to Peter Gay's brilliant biography puts it. Freud is more than an 'Everyman' whose life mirrors our own concerns. By postulating the unconscious, Freud shifts attention from the surface features of life to that which lies beneath. In making this shift, Freud allows a glimpse of all human lives as fascinating and far from mundane. The meaning of a life is not understood merely through considering its history in the 'real' world of activities and events. The 'success' of a life cannot be assessed simply by considering its impact upon the political or social scene. Allowing the unconscious (and by implication the secret and internal processes of our lives) to take centre stage means that all lives are fascinating, regardless of their events, because the content of our unconscious – our fears, desires, and phantasies, and the way in which they help construct our responses to the world – is unique to each and every one.

Nietzsche, that shadowy presence in Freud's writing, noted that 'Man' may not be 'the crown of creation'; indeed 'he is relatively speaking, the most unsuccessful animal, the sickliest, the one most dangerously strayed from its instincts' – but 'with all that, to be sure, [he is] the most interesting!' Freud would no doubt have agreed. In this book, that idea will be pursued by investigating four key themes in Freud's writing that have the ability to challenge and shape the way in which we understand ourselves. Through considering his ideas on hysteria, the Oedipus complex and sexuality, dreams and the unconscious, and religion, we will, I hope, gain a sense of how Freud's theories and practices allow for the development of a perspective on life that is both rich and fascinating.

Freud's ideas begin with the attempt to understand mental illness but they end with a much wider discussion of the forces and attitudes that make up human life. The breadth of this endeavour of itself makes reading Freud worthwhile. There is, however, a further dimension to consider as we encounter Freud and his work. What is presented is not just another theory but a set of reflective practices and ideas that make it possible for us all to find more fulfilling ways of living.

2

Hysteria and the development of psychoanalysis

As we begin to explore Freud's ideas in more detail, we will do well to remember that his theories are grounded in reflections on his clinical practice. His account of the mind is shaped by his practical experience of working with people suffering from incapacitating neurotic illness: that is, mental disorders which affected their ability to function. To ignore the practical context for his ideas would be a mistake, not least because his approach to defining the human is both innovative and controversial, emerging from his clinical work with those who are 'sick'.

'Sickness' and 'health' are not polar opposites for Freud. There is a significant connection between the experiences and practices of those who are mentally sick and those who are mentally healthy. When Freud seeks to understand hysteria – the illness which formed the basis for his early clinical work – he does not see the hysteric as standing apart in her 'madness' from other human beings. 'Her' suffering (as we shall see, the hysteric was invariably female) and the solutions that she finds to her problems are simply more extreme versions of the solutions that other (apparently 'healthy') human beings employ to make sense of their lives, albeit in rather different ways.

The hysteric holds an important place in the history of psychoanalysis, not least because through his work with hysterics Freud comes to develop crucial aspects of psychoanalytic thought and practice. Freud's earliest clinical work was in relation to hysteria; thus it makes sense to start here. More than that: through his work with these patients, Freud develops the distinctive nature of his method and theory. Straight away, this suggests something of the innovation of his approach, for the theory he develops comes out of his relationship with these patients. The partnership between analyst and patient is what makes therapy a distinctive practice. As the French analyst Jacques Lacan describes it, psychoanalysis is 'a dialectical experience'; in other words, it consists of a conversation between two people. The patient is far from passive; exploring the therapeutic relationship between Freud and the hysterics whom he attempts to treat reveals something of the triumphs and pitfalls of that messy (and very human) process.

A 'hystory' of hysteria

Freud's first patients were women suffering from hysteria. Drawn from well-to-do Viennese families, Freud sought to cure these patients of the debilitating symptoms that limited their ability to function in the world. As well as seeking to cure them, he sought to understand the sources of their illness and the experiences that had led to the peculiar symptoms from which they suffered.

Freud's desire to understand the sources of hysteria led him to formulate many of his theories; talking with his patients challenged some of his initial thoughts about the origins of hysteria. At first, he thought that hysteria resulted from a response to a traumatic event, often an attempted, or real, sexual seduction by an adult. As Freud worked with his patients, he came to a rather different conclusion, believing that hysteria is best understood as a psychological response to an unacceptable desire.

Freud's rejection of the idea that abuse accounts for hysteria has led to much criticism. Some have accused him of denying the reality of child abuse and replacing it with a theory that sees the child imagining instances of abuse. In a letter to Wilhelm Fliess, written in September 1897, Freud wrote that 'I no longer believe in my neurotica'. That he no longer believes in his patients' stories of childhood seduction sounds damning, to say the least. However, we should note that Freud recognizes the role of sexual abuse in the development of mental illness, most notably in the case of the Wolf Man, who Freud accepts was seduced as a young child by his older sister. Freud's concern, as we shall see, is to move the discussion of hysteria away from discussion of external events towards a discussion of the internal processes that shape hysterical symptoms. It may well be that in making this move he fails to engage adequately with the way in which experiences of the world beyond the patient shape the patient's illness.

When writing up his ideas on hysteria, Freud uses case studies of his patients, a method that caused him some consternation. These studies are, by their very nature, dramatic and read less like the reports of level-headed, empirical investigations and more like a series of short stories (Freud, 1905a: 9). Yet what causes Freud the scientist to feel uneasy, we – his readers – may respond to rather differently. The intensely personal and intimate nature of the case studies reveals psychoanalysis to be a peculiar practice. It engages with individual experience but it also involves a relationship between two parties. Because its practice and theory emerge from the conversation between analyst and patient, the tale that unfolds in the consulting room is not straightforwardly lineal: it meanders, it changes. The patient may come to different interpretations of the same events at different points in the analysis, or indeed after it. This makes psychoanalysis somewhat problematic for the scientist, as its shifting processes do not fit easily with a model of scientific practice as lineal and logical.

If the style of the case study disquieted Freud, the very application of the term 'hysteria' is similarly fraught. In the history of misogyny, the construction of hysteria as a form of illness stands out as one way in which the loathing of women and their bodies has been most powerfully expressed. Associated only with women, the Ancient Greeks understood hysteria to be, literally, a complaint of the womb. It was thought that a woman became 'hysterical' because her womb was wandering round her body. The only remedy for such an illness was to ensure that the sufferer was safely under the control of a man, be that her husband or her father. Behind such accounts lies the common association of women with that which is irrational: an idea that dogs women well beyond the era of the Greeks. Femininity and femaleness have been defined throughout western history in dismissive and condemnatory ways; the symptoms of hysteria and the way in which it has been understood have lent weight to those unflattering constructions. In the Christian era, almost any kind of unruly female behaviour was called 'hysteria', which was then connected with various forms of immoral behaviour. Not until the seventeenth century was hysteria seen to be less a problem of the womb and more a disease of the nervous system. In the nineteenth century, the medical and moral accounts of hysteria were strangely combined to argue that the hysteric's illness was grounded in degeneracy. The hysteric was both physically and morally sick.

Not surprisingly, feminists have argued that hysteria can only be understood against the backdrop of the history of women's oppression. While some note it to be symptomatic of that broader oppressive history, others see it less as an illness and more as a strategy for resistance. Being a hysteric brought a degree of power and autonomy in a society in which women had precious little of either. The disruptive power of hysteria – think of the symptoms described in the previous chapter – would be felt throughout the home. The woman whose body is wracked by strange pains, who cannot speak, eat, or drink, will not be able to concern herself with domestic chores and household management. The disabling aspect of the illness means that the stifling routines of domesticity will necessarily be broken, the patterns of the home being forced to conform to the contours of the illness. Hysteria read in this way becomes a kind of victory for the woman suffering from it.

Such readings make sense; we should note that Freud also identifies the 'secondary function' of illness, used by the sufferer to achieve some benefit (Freud, 1905a: 42–3). However, it is important not to ignore the debilitating aspect of hysterical ill-ness. The freedom from routine acquired in a hysterical bout could just as well lead to the sufferer being institutionalized. Even if we accept the construction of hysteria as reflecting historical attitudes to women, the symptoms that make it up are far from absent in the contemporary world and are still encountered in the illnesses that have taken its place. As the Lacanian psychoana-lyst Lionel Bailly points out, just because hysteria is no longer in the diagnostic manuals, does not mean that it no longer exists. Similarly, the British analyst Christopher Bollas identifies the ghost of the hysteric in eating disorders and the fatigue of ME.

At the time Freud opens his practice, Jean-Martin Charcot's work, emphasising the material basis of hysteria, was suggesting the possibility of a more sympathetic engagement with the hys-teric than had been the case. Charcot believed hysteria to be a disturbance of the nervous system, based in heredity. This meant that, at least in theory, hysteria lost its gendered nature, for both women and men could be hysterics. Charcot's attempts at treat-ing the condition made use of hypnosis, both as a way of replicat-ing the hysterical attack but also to introduce suggestions to the hysteric that might enable a cure. This had an unintended effect: the hysterical attack could be reproduced for a medical audience and thus hysteria became a form of performance that could be marvelled at by others. In the past the hysteric had been a silent presence; Charcot now encouraged her to tell her story. However, he tended to see her words as another symptom to be analysed and invariably that meant not taking too seriously the things that she said. As Julia Borossa notes, 'the hysteric could indeed speak – she was even heard – but still she was far from being listened to'.

Psychoanalytic method and *Studies on Hysteria*

Against this backdrop, Freud's work – first with his friend and mentor Josef Breuer and then in his own practice – formed the basis for a radically different approach to hysterical illness. *Studies on Hysteria* (1893–5) offers the case studies of five hysterics suffering a variety of physical symptoms for which no physical reason could be found. These symptoms included hydrophobia (the fear of water, accompanied by the inability to drink) and limb paralysis. As well as providing fascinating insights into the phenomena that accompany hysteria, the *Studies* also show Freud's personal and professional transition. He stops being a physician offering physiological accounts of neurotic illness and becomes one who bases his practice on the search for psychological causes and solutions. The research biologist becomes the psychologist. Engaging with these early reflections on neurotic illness also suggests something of the collaborative nature of psychoanalysis, for the experiences of the hysterics with whom Freud works comes to shape the development of his psychoanalytic practice.

The clinical practice detailed in the *Studies on Hysteria* stems from Breuer's 'cathartic method'. In this method, therapeutic suggestions were made to the hysterical patient whilst they were under hypnosis. Breuer builds upon Charcot's use of hypnosis. But Breuer went further: under hypnosis, symptoms were traced to their source. This was a significant development, for once the source of the symptom was identified, its power to affect the hysteric's actions was undermined and the symptom disappeared.

Breuer's most famous patient was 'Anna O'. (Anna's real name was Bertha Pappenheim; throughout this chapter the pseudonyms Freud and Breuer applied to maintain their patients' anonymity will be used.) One of Anna's most troubling symptoms was that she could not drink water. By employing his cathartic method, Breuer was able to help her trace this symptom back to an experience of seeing her lady companion's dog drinking from a glass of water: an action that she found disgusting. Identifying this source of her symptom enabled her to drink once again (Breuer and Freud, 1893–5: 34–5).

This practical result led to an advance in Breuer and Freud's theories about what caused hysteria. Symptoms were not random and without meaning but were bodily expressions of psychic trauma. The emotional energy attached to a traumatic event did not find expression through normal physical processes but was blocked; this 'abreaction' becomes the basis for the development of the pathological symptom. While Freud moves beyond this interpretation in his later thinking, at this stage it is important to note the way in which the relationship between doctor and patient is significant for determining the success or otherwise of the treatment. A cure was dependent upon the patient remembering and expressing the trauma that formed the basis of the symptom's construction. The very emphasis on talking this through placed considerable weight on the quality of the relationship between patient and doctor. Did the patient trust the doctor enough to share her reminiscences with him? For a cure to be found, the hysteric's voice had to be heard. Could (would?) the doctor hear what she was saying?

The alliance between doctor and patient needed for treating the illness becomes even more important as Freud develops his own method. Breuer's cathartic method depended upon the use of hypnosis as the means by which symptoms could be traced to their source. Increasingly, Freud found this practice less than useful; mainly because he encountered patients for whom hypnosis was not particularly helpful or who could not be easily hypnotized. Whether this deficiency lay with the patient or his own lack of talent as a hypnotist, Freud was not sure. Whatever the case, Emmy von N's difficulties with being hypnotized led him to seek an alternative method.

'Emmy von N' (real name Fanny Moser) was the wealthy widow of a much older husband. Much gossip had greeted her husband's death, including rumours that the young woman had murdered her husband. Plagued by depression, insomnia, halluci-nations, and bodily pains and tics, she became Freud's patient in 1889. Emmy's treatment was not easy, not least because Freud found it difficult to hypnotize her. Others might have thrown up their hands in despair and decided she was incurable. Freud's response was different and led to a major development in his clinical practice. Realizing that what was most important in her treatment was what she told him before being hypnotized, he starts to consider whether hypnosis is necessary for his practice. Talking to him seems more effective, as it is only those symptoms subjected to this 'psychical analysis' that were permanently removed (Breuer and Freud, 1893–5: 101).

At this stage, Freud does not feel comfortable giving up hypnosis entirely. In Emmy's case, he even uses hypnosis to play a trick on her. Perhaps picking up on Freud's doubts, Emmy expresses scepticism about the efficacy of the suggestions that Freud makes to her while she is under hypnosis. Freud hypnotizes her and gives her a note, telling her that:

> At lunch today you will pour me out a glass of red wine, just as you did yesterday. As I raise the glass to my lips you will say: 'Oh, please pour me out a glass too', and when I reach for the bottle, you will say: 'No thank you, I don't think I will after all.' You will then put your hand in your bag, draw out the piece of paper and find those same words written on it (Breuer and Freud, 1893–5: 84–5).

He reports with triumph that 'the little episode took place exactly as I had pre-arranged it'; Emmy stared at her doctor in astonishment as she read the note (Breuer and Freud, 1893–5: 85). The power of the physician to manipulate his patient is foremost in this little scene, revealing the one-sided nature of the relationship between doctor and patient when it involves the application of hypnosis. As we watch Freud develop his method, it is important to question the extent to which psychoanalytic therapy retains this power imbalance.

In the treatment of 'Elisabeth von R' (Breuer and Freud, 1893–5: 135–81), Freud dispenses with hypnosis altogether. 'Elisabeth' (Ilona Weiss) was suffering from pains in her legs and had difficulty in walking. Having determined that the problem was not physical, Freud looks for a psychical cure for her suffering. In place of hypnosis, he relies on what he has come to call the 'concentration' technique. To understand the complex series of experiences that have led to the pains in her legs, Freud makes her lie down (the famous couch enters the psychoanalytic scene) and close her eyes. Applying pressure to her forehead, he asks her to report faithfully whatever comes into her mind. She does so and a terribly sad tale of unrequited love emerges. In love with her brother-in-law, her immediate response to her beloved sister's death is to realize that he is now free to marry her. This 'unacceptable thought' challenges everything that she believes about herself as a moral, upright, loving, and loyal person. She resists it and forces it out of consciousness. In its place the symptom of pain in her legs is produced. This symptom is traced back to the very walks that she had enjoyed with her brother-in-law before the death of her sister. Determined to resist the pleasure that she found in his company, her legs become a source of punishment for her unacceptable thoughts. The unacceptable thought is rejected, resisted, and – though apparently forgotten – turned upon the self. No wonder Freud notes that, far from being the degenerate fiends of popular myth, invariably the hysteric is too moral, punishing herself for her unacceptable desires (Breuer and Freud, 1893–5: 161). For Elisabeth, healing involves recovering the thought and accepting it. The disappearance of the symptom has a most pleasing postscript, which Freud describes:

> In the spring of 1894 I heard that she was going to a private ball for which I was able to get an invitation and I did not allow the opportunity to escape me of seeing my former patient whirl past me in a lively dance (Breuer and Freud, 1893–95: 160).

The concentration technique, it seems, was therapeutically far more effective than hypnosis. Importantly, the hysteric's voice is not only being heard but is also shaping the narrative. The concentration method in time becomes the bedrock for psychoanalytic therapy: free association. The patient is not to censor her thoughts. Whatever she thinks is to be discussed with the doctor, however unimportant, wild, or even immoral it might seem. All ideas are followed through; their connections to other events and feelings, explored. During this process it is not for the physician to decide what is and is not relevant: the patient must shape the discourse. As Freud notes, trying to 'cut to the chase' does not work.

Having sought to dispense quickly with Emmy von N's fears concerning the practices in lunatic asylums (fears that seemed to have little to do with what Freud suspected lay at the heart of her condition), Freud realised that seeking to make the patient accept a 'rational' and logical reading of their troubles simply did not work. 'I cannot evade listening to her stories in every detail to the very end,' he writes (Breuer and Freud, 1893–5: 61). Emmy needed to speak about her fears. And when these apparently irrelevant fears were discussed, new avenues for understanding the sickness opened up. Analysing what seemed irrelevant was just as important as analysing what the doctor thought was relevant. The doctor is, then, far from omniscient in determining the shape of the discussions between 'himself' and the patient. The therapeutic setting, if it is to be effective, has to be understood as a partnership.

The *Studies on Hysteria* suggest the positive impact that cultivating the relationship between doctor and patient might have for therapy. Arguably the most important advance for Freud's theory comes through the experience of an analysis in which the relationship between Freud and his patient is anything but successful. In the figure of Dora, the hysteric is far from a benign and pliable conversation partner. Her analysis is a failure, yet by attempting to understand what went wrong Freud formulates a significant aspect of psychoanalytic therapy.

Shaping psychoanalytic theory: Dora and transference

The fragmentary analysis of Ida Bauer (or 'Dora') is one of the most important case studies for the development of psychoanalysis. Dora's story is a sad and disturbing one. Brought to Freud by her father in 1900, she had suffered since the age of eight from a range of symptoms that had no identifiable physiological cause: dyspnoea (difficulty in breathing), headaches, a nervous cough, and loss of voice. At the time of her first meeting Freud, she is suffering from 'low spirits' and has entertained suicidal thoughts. She has also made upsetting allegations against a family friend – 'Herr K' – who she claims propositioned her during a walk. Herr K vehemently denies this allegation and Dora's father is less than sympathetic to his daughter, believing that this proposition is a 'phantasy that has forced its way into her mind' (Freud, 1905a: 26). He asks Freud to 'bring [Dora] to reason' (Freud, 1905a: 26). In this respect, the analysis starts against the backdrop of the pattern established by Charcot: the 'irrational' hysteric is to be brought to her senses by the 'reasonable' physician.

Freud's account of Dora's analysis is fascinating and reads like precisely the kind of titillating novella about which Freud was so uneasy when using the form of the case study. A complicated quadrille of relationships is uncovered. The wife of her attempted seducer – 'Frau K' – is also her father's lover. Dora has come to believe (with good reason) that her father intends her to become Herr K's lover so that his own liaison may continue. Seen in this light, Dora's symptoms can be read as a perfectly natural response to an unacceptable state of affairs: her illness results from her extreme unhappiness at being used as a pawn in others' sexual games. Feminist discussions of Dora's case argue strongly for such a reading: women are made ill by the system of patriarchal control and abuse that renders them powerless. At the same time, Freud has (rightly) been criticized for failing to attend adequately to the effects that the stratagems of the people surrounding Dora have on her.

Initially, it seems surprising that Freud does not spend more time considering the impact of Dora's actual relationships. Freud's aim is to get Dora to focus on her desires and how her refusal to acknowledge them is making her ill. The focus he proposes, as he starts to treat her, involves shifting the gaze from the external world to the internal world. Psychoanalysis remains controversial to this day because of this move inwards. By making this shift, does it ignore the problems of social inequality and the kind of abuses people inflict on each other? As we follow Dora's case, it is worth asking whether Freud's method inevitably downplays the reality of the abusive relationships to which Dora is subjected. More broadly, we might also ask whether the psychoanalytic method places sufficient weight on one's circumstances when the therapist seeks to access the individual's complex range of feelings in response to such abusive experiences. Whatever our conclusions, Freud's attempt to consider Dora's desires results in part from his rejection of his initial theory for understanding hysteria as an illness which results from a traumatic event. In his attempt to map the unconscious, his attention shifts from the events that shape hysterical symptoms towards the unacknowledged desires that he claims drive the hysteric.

The analysis starts promisingly, probably because Freud does not take Dora's father's version of events at face value (Freud, 1905a: 26). The shape of the analysis seems to be in Dora's hands. This is implied by Freud's description of how the method of free association works, which he places at the beginning of her case study: 'I now let the patient himself choose the subject of the day's work and in that way I start out from whatever surface his unconscious happens to be presenting to his notice at the moment' (Freud, 1905a: 12). Such an approach – less determined, more 'piecemeal' (Freud, 1905a: 12) – suggests that the patient shapes the analysis, not the doctor. In adopting this method, the insights gained from the analysis of Emmy von N are clearly being built on.

The application of this method to Dora's treatment seems to be going well, until, without warning, she breaks off the analysis. Freud is shocked; he had no idea that this was coming. Determined to discover why she has done this, his reflections lead him to identify a phenomenon that will, in the hands of later analysts like Melanie Klein, become one of the most important aspects of psychoanalytic practice: the transference. Freud defines transference as:

> New editions or facsimiles of the impulses and phantasies which are aroused and made conscious during the progress of the analysis; but they have this peculiarity, which is characteristic for their species, that they replace some earlier person by the person of the physician (Freud, 1905a: 116).

In the case of Dora, Freud encounters the power of this phenomenon in the fundamentally hostile identification or transference that she makes between him and her father. Failing to identify this hostility, Freud is shocked by the way in which the analysis ends. Perhaps it would not have come as such a shock if he had recognized that Dora had made this connection. Dora desires – unsurprisingly – to take revenge against the father she loves and yet who has delivered her to his lover's husband. Freud has come to represent her father and so, without warning, she breaks off the analysis; a certain way of causing her doctor/father pain! To his credit, Freud refuses to ignore what this case might suggest about his practice, accepting that he has failed to identify the hostile connection on which Dora acts with such power. Before we get too carried away, however, it is important to recognize that while some important clinical reflections come from this case, Freud did not escape altogether unscathed from his encounter with Dora. Indeed, in many ways, the aftermath of this analysis may well have limited Freud's ability to adequately engage with the negative aspects of the analyst/patient relationship.

Sex, phantasy, and hysteria

Shifting his attention from the external to the internal dimension of the patient's experience opens up discussion of the relationship between what we might call the 'inner' and 'outer' worlds of the hysteric's experience.

This relationship is most obviously played out in the role that sex plays. A common feature of the cases that Freud presents is the failure of the hysteric to feel comfortable with sex in 'the real world'. That does not, however, mean that she is without desire. In the psychoanalytic theories that develop after Freud, a distinction is sometimes made between 'phantasy' as unconscious desire and 'fantasy' as something consciously shaped and played with and that connects to the work of imagination and creativity. In point of fact, there is an overlap between the two, as the contemporary psychoanalysts Jean Laplanche and Jean-Bertrand

Pontalis have suggested. What matters is that 'reality' is not the only plain on which we play out our lives. Powerful imaginative connections also shape our experience and these may be activities of which we are conscious or unconscious. In Dora's case, unconscious connections and sexual phantasies are played out on her body in the form of her symptoms.

After suffering appendicitis, Dora was not able to walk properly, dragging her leg: a symptom that could not be accounted for by her doctors. Initially, Freud assumes (with her doctors) that her appendicitis is not a hysterical symptom. He becomes less convinced when he starts to question Dora about it and the way it relates to her dragging leg. When did it happen? Nine months after Dora had been propositioned by Herr K. 'Nine months' suggests pregnancy; Freud interprets this as an indication that, despite Dora's protestations to the contrary, she would have liked to accept Herr K's advances. Had she done so, this could have led to birth pangs rather than the pains of appendicitis. How might this relate to the dragging leg? Freud asks if she had hurt her leg before. Yes, in childhood, when she twisted her ankle while going downstairs. In other words, she had made 'a false step' and the symptom now reflects her disappointment at not having accepted Herr K. 'In your unconscious you must have regretted the upshot of the scene' (Freud, 1905a: 104). In creating the symptoms of appendicitis and the dragging leg, Dora is able to play out the results of the sexual encounter that she has rejected.

Dora's case is not the only one where the connection between sexual phantasy and symptom is apparent. We might return to Breuer's patient, Anna O. At the time of her treatment, possible connections between her symptoms and her sexual desires were not explored. Years later, Freud claims that this was a telling failure on Breuer's part; moreover, it was a failure to engage with the sexual realm that distorted Breuer's account of the analysis. In the *Studies* Breuer claims that Anna attained a 'final cure' (Breuer and

Freud, 1893–5: 47). Freud, however, disputes this, suggesting that the end of the analysis was disrupted by an unidentified transference to Breuer that was clearly sexual.

This is Freud's account of the end of Anna's analysis. Breuer did not realize that Anna was in love with him and he is horrified when she declares that she is pregnant with his child. Anna was not pregnant but, shocked by her phantasy of a relationship with him, Breuer ends her treatment. The revelation of the power of the unconscious identification that she has made with him was too much for Breuer.

If we return to the analysis with Dora, Freud may well, like Breuer, fail to recognize what is going on for the patient but at least he attempts to engage with the aftermath of an analysis that has broken down. If Breuer was unable – or unwilling – to engage with the sexual nature of Anna's perception of him, Freud's concern to engage with Dora's phantasies shifts the discussion of hysteria explicitly into the sexual realm.

While the later theory of analysts such as Melanie Klein claims all human relationships are subject to the interplay between phantasy and reality, exploring the particular way in which the hysteric inhabits the world of phantasy allows the role of unconscious forces to be made evident. During 1881–2, Anna O's 'absences' – periods when she is completely detached from the world around her – involve the phantasy of reliving the events of 1880–1 (Breuer and Freud, 1893–5: 33). The 'real' world is rejected in favour of the past. Preferring this world of phantasy to the real world, it is not surprising that some kind of transference will be made towards the doctor; and that transference is likely to be erotic. In Dora's case, the desire for revenge drives her actions, both in reality and in the analytic setting. Love and hate can be at work in the transference, making it a powerful (sometimes destructive) element of an analysis that is not always easy to identify: a fact attested by the case's conclusion.

In Dora's case

Freud may turn his attention to the role of phantasy in this case
but that does not mean that he ignores Dora's circumstances
completely. The problem, perhaps, is that he focuses too much on
her relationship with her father to the detriment of an adequate
analysis of her other relationships. He also reads this father/
daughter relationship in terms of the other theory that he is
developing during this time (see Freud, 1900: 122–33, 256), which
we will consider in more detail in the next chapter: the Oedipus
complex.

In considering Dora's family, Freud begins by noting 'the
usual sexual attraction' (Freud, 1905a: 21) that exists between
father and daughter and mother and son. This is a straightforward,
clear description of the central claim of the Oedipus complex:
the child desires the parent of the opposite sex. At the same time,
he outlines the complex relationship among Dora and her father,
his lover and her husband, which also shapes her circumstances.
Surprisingly, given Dora's circumstances, he doesn't fall back on
the theory that shaped his work with Breuer. Then, he saw hysteria as arising from a psychic trauma (Freud, 1905a: 26–7; also
Freud, 1896). Transferred to this case, it would be a relatively easy
step to see Herr K's attempted seduction as the cause of Dora's
hysterical symptoms. But Freud challenges the 'simplicity' of that
diagnosis. In Dora's case he feels there is good evidence that the
attempted seduction itself was 'insufficient' to 'determine the
particular character of the symptoms' (Freud, 1905a: 27). After all,
many of Dora's symptoms date from long before the events with
Herr K. To find a solution, Freud decides that he needs to access
the realm of Dora's unconscious and that necessitates using dream
analysis.

In Chapter 4 we will consider how Freud understands dreams
as allowing access to the unconscious. For now, it is sufficient to
note that Freud sees dreams as one of the most powerful tools for

accessing the hidden world of the unconscious. In dreams, wishes are revealed. In dreams, it is possible for that which has been rendered unconscious to evade the processes of repression (Freud, 1905a: 15). As Freud notes in a letter to his friend Wilhelm Fliess in January 1899, this is of particular benefit when attempting to understand hysteria, for 'the key to hysteria ... lies in dreams'.

What do Dora's dreams suggest about the nature of her unconscious desires? Freud highlights two of her dreams to suggest something of the nature of Dora's phantasies. The first dream is short and to the point and recurred over three nights after Herr K's attempted seduction:

> A house was on fire. My father was standing beside my bed and woke me up. I dressed quickly. Mother wanted to stop and save her jewel-case; but Father said: 'I refuse to let myself and my two children be burnt for the sake of your jewel-case.' We hurried downstairs and as soon as I was outside I woke up (Freud, 1905a: 64).

Freud asks Dora to free associate around the dream's contents. Working with her associations he comes to the following (rather confident) interpretation of her dream. The jewel-box (a common symbol for female genitals) is not her mother's but her own. In resisting her feelings for Herr K, she has summoned up her old Oedipal love for her father. Interpreted thus, the dream reveals that:

> You are ready to give Herr K what his wife withholds from him. That is the thought that has to be repressed with so much energy and which has made it necessary for every one of its elements to be turned into its opposite (Freud, 1905a: 70).

Dora, not surprisingly, rejects this interpretation. The second dream is more complicated and, as we shall see, Freud neglects to consider those parts of the dream that relate to him. Here is the dream as Dora tells it:

> I was walking about in a town which I did not know. I saw streets and squares which were strange to me. Then I came into a house where I lived, went to my room and found a letter from Mother lying there. She wrote saying that as I had left home without my parents' knowledge she had not wished to write to me to say that Father was ill. 'Now he is dead and if you like you can come.' I thus went to the station and asked about a hundred times: 'Where is the station?' I always got the answer: 'Five minutes.' I then saw a thick wood before me which I went into and there I asked a man whom I met. He said to me: 'Two and a half hours more.' He offered to accompany me. But I refused and went alone. I saw the station in front of me and could not reach it. At the same time I had the usual feeling of anxiety that one has in dreams when one cannot move forward. Then I was at home. I walked into the porter's lodge and enquired after our flat. The maidservant opened the door to me and replied that Mother and the others were already at the cemetery (Freud, 1905a: 94).

Initially, Freud focuses on the parts of the dream that suggest Dora's craving for revenge: she is living apart from her family; her father is dead. Her father's death would be something liberating, for then she could do as she pleased. Yet the dream also points closer to home; a fact that Freud realizes only when it is too late and the analysis has broken down. When the dream refers to 'two and a half hours more', Dora is giving Freud notice that she intends to finish the analysis. She is effectively saying that she has 'only two and half hours more *with Freud*'. Dora has dealt with Freud as a woman of her class might well deal with a servant: she has given him a fortnight's notice (a fact that clearly rankles with the learned physician).

Freud's shock is understandable, to a degree. He thinks that he has given Dora space to tell her story; he has not given much credence to her father's claims. Yet Freud has not listened closely enough to what Dora has to say. Remember Lacan's claim that psychoanalysis is a dialogue between two parties. Because two parties are involved, it is not surprising that there may be misunderstanding and imbalance. Freud may listen to Dora's story but he tends to use what she says to confirm his increasing belief that the Oedipus complex is the fundamental infantile experience that shapes human sexuality. Given this obsession, it is not surprising that Freud sees Dora's relationship with her father as the most important factor for determining the roots of her hysteria: hence his interpretation of the first dream in terms of Dora's Oedipal phantasy of her father (Freud, 1905a: 86). This interpretation pays insufficient attention to the role of Dora's mother in this dream; after all, the mother's jewel-case lies at its heart. This image suggests something important about Dora's identification with the women that surround her: an identification that Freud, increasingly concerned with masculine figures, consigns to the footnotes of the case.

Neglecting Dora's female relationships reflects Freud's focus on male sexual development. As he develops his ideas on the Oedipus complex, he assumes, at least at this stage in his enquiries, that this idea of sexual attraction can be applied, by a simple reversal, to women as well as men. Women want to remove the mother, in order to take possession of the father (Freud, 1916–17: 333). Freud reads Dora as providing plenty of evidence for this theory. For example, Freud identifies her nervous cough as a phantasy of fellatio performed on her father by Frau K. Freud reads this as Dora identifying with her father's lover, thus taking her mother's place in phantasy, just as surely as Frau K has in reality (Freud, 1905a: 56). Later, Freud develops a more complex account of female sexual development; to return to the first identification with the mother, the girl must reject the father (Freud, 1924b).

This rejection, for the later Freud, is based on the father's failure to provide the girl with a child: the child acting as a substitute for the penis that the girl believes she lacks. Dora's revenge on her father for having failed her could then be seen as grounded on a similar sense of disappointment.

The desire for revenge against the father ultimately shapes the transference that Dora makes to Freud. As one reads the case study it is interesting to note the extent to which Freud under-estimates the power of her anger. He is undoubtedly aware, to some degree, of her rage. There is a purifying quality to it – rather like the fire of a furnace – that means that when Dora talks of her father's affair there are none of the usual gaps in her recollections. She is lucid and forthcoming. As Freud notes these associations, the reader gets a sense of her justifiable anger at being offered as a sexual sacrifice to facilitate her father's affair (Freud, 1905a: 32). Indeed, Freud agrees that she is right to feel bitter about being used in this way (Freud, 1905a: 34). But because he tends to see the desire for her father's love as the background to such feelings he fails to engage adequately with her anger. He even suggests that if her father gave up Frau K for her sake, leaving Dora victorious, she would be healed (Freud, 1905a: 42).

Underestimating her hostility has implications for how Freud engages with the transference that Dora makes to him. He notes the connection Dora makes between him and her father: Freud, her father and Herr K are all 'passionate smokers' (Freud, 1905a: 73). However, he tends to read this identification less as providing a link between him and her father and more as evidence of an identification between himself and Herr K. Just as he sees Dora being tempted by Herr K's kiss, so he imagines that she would like a kiss from him (Freud, 1905a: 74). For Freud, Herr K is a romantic figure for Dora. She may direct much of her anger at her would-be seducer but her deeper rage is against her father's betrayal. At one point Freud believes that he has enabled Dora to accept that she loved Herr K (Freud, 1905a: 104) but this is a deceptive moment. By focusing on the identification of Herr K as Dora's desired lover and then connecting himself with this prospective lover, Freud primarily identifies transference-love at work in Dora's relationship with him. In other words, the love Dora feels for Herr K (or at least the love that Freud identifies) is projected on to Freud in the analysis.

This rather romantic illusion suggests something of Freud's own weaknesses; in this case grounded in his tendency to think about women within the bourgeois constructions of his age. In a letter to his daughter Mathilde, he describes the qualities of a good wife: 'gentleness, cheerfulness and the talent to make ... life easier and more beautiful'. Thinking of women in this rather idealized way may have contributed to the difficulties he has in identifying the anger, jealousy, and hate that drive Dora's hysteria and its motivations.

The deeper transference-hate is only identified when the analysis reaches its premature conclusion. As we have seen, Freud subsequently reads Dora's second dream as announcing her intent to break off the analysis. This dream confronts Freud with the significance of Dora's desire for revenge. Dreaming of her father's death suggests 'a phantasy of revenge directed against her father' (Freud, 1905a: 110 footnote 1). Yet as he moves, oblivious, towards the end of the analysis, Freud remains blind to the fact that Dora is obsessed with revenge, maintaining that love is her prime concern. Confronting Dora with her continued love for Herr K, he notes with satisfaction that 'Dora disputed the fact no longer' (Freud, 1905a: 104).

Only in the final session does Freud realize the extent to which the desire for revenge determines her relationships. Having declared that this is the final session, she goes on to say the things that Freud has not been willing to hear. Contrary to appearances, she was not offended by Herr K's attempt to seduce her. What offended her was the knowledge that he had seduced the K's governess in a similar fashion (Freud, 1905a: 106). Did Herr K really believe that she would be so common as to accept him like some lowly servant? This 'betrayal' amplifies the deeper betrayal of her father. In this context, the transference to Freud as lover masks the transference to Freud as father. Dora's revenge – brought about by rejecting Freud – hits its mark: 'Her breaking off so unexpectedly, just when my hopes of a successful termination of the treatment were at their highest and her thus bringing those hopes to nothing – this was an unmistakable act of vengeance on her part' (Freud, 1905a: 109).

The literary critic Steven Marcus suggests that Freud was fixated with the possibility of a 'happy ending' for Dora, in which she could accept Herr K and, eventually, become his wife (Freud, 1905a: 107–8). Dora, however, has a different ending in mind; an ending which reveals that the power of love does not always overcome the power of hate. The desire for revenge, played out in the analytic setting, is given full expression some years later in the real world. One of the Ks' children has died. Dora takes the opportunity to call on them to offer her condolences and to reconcile. This act of reconciliation provides the context for her revenge. She tells Frau K she knows of her affair with her father; she gets Herr K to admit that he had indeed tried to seduce her and she confronts her father, thus instigating a break with her family (Freud, 1905a: 121). Freud notes that she does not see the Ks again.

Our sympathies may well lie with Dora. She has taken matters into her own hands and is no longer a passive plaything, at the mercy of the machinations of others. There is, however, a surprising epilogue, which suggests a rather more complex state of affairs. It also hints at Freud's failure to pay adequate attention to the relationship between Dora and Frau K. Even within the parameters of Freud's description of the case, there are details that suggest a deep friendship – perhaps more – between the two women, details that Freud singularly fails to consider when seeking to identify Dora's unconscious yearnings. Some years later,

Dora and Frau K meet again, and become bridge partners. This re-emergence of their relationship suggests a deeper connection between them than Freud – fixed on exploring heterosexual Oedipal relationships – could imagine. This is how Lisa Appignanesi and John Forrester describe the new-found relationship between Dora and Frau K:

> It is as if, across the years, they [Dora and Frau K] had finally dispensed with the superfluous men who had previously been their partners in their complex social games and contracts, yet they had retained their love of those games whose skill lies in the secret of mutual understanding of open yet coded communications within and across a foursome. [Dora], adept at keeping her hand secret, also knew when and how to play it. One can only guess at the complexity of that particular partnership.

Dora's ghost: the hysteric and psychoanalytic theory

If we were to consider only Freud's explicit references to Dora in his later work we might be left thinking that this failed analysis had little impact on his theorizing. This is not the case. Dora seems to haunt Freud: his last paper, indeed, sees him engaging with the notion of whether there can ever be a 'successful' (in the sense of complete) analysis, suggesting that he was grappling with this most famous of unsuccessful cases to the very end (Freud, 1937a).

In his concluding comments on Dora's case, Freud makes some initial remarks about the transference (Freud, 1905a: 116–20) and picks up this theme again some years later in his theoretical papers on technique (Freud, 1912 and 1915a). These papers suggest significant ways in which his relationship with Dora informed his thinking on the nature of transference.

In *The Dynamics of Transference* (1912), Freud begins by noting transference as a form of resistance on the part of the patient. By projecting powerful erotic desires on to the analyst, the source of these feelings, in the patient's earliest relationships, can be hidden. The patient is convinced that their feelings come about as a result of the person of the analyst, rather than seeing them as repetitions of past attachments (Freud, 1912: 104). Both erotic and hostile forms of transference resist the necessity of using the analysis to engage with one's past and particularly the identifications that have shaped one's sense of self. I might, for example, deny the need to discuss the role of my father in my early life, and my feelings for him, by fantasising instead about my male analyst. Such feelings might seem 'real' but in practice they act as a distraction from the emotionally tiring work of analysis. I am caught up in the passion of a crush, rather than engaging with the difficult feelings I have about my father. The notion of transference as distraction suggests that nothing positive can be derived from these projections of emotion. However, Freud notes that a positive transference to the analyst can be helpful for treatment. Feelings of 'sympathy, friendship, trust and the like' (Freud, 1912: 105) can advance the analysis.

Such emotions were, it would seem, lacking in Freud's relationship with Dora, and not just on her side. If Dora seeks to take her revenge on Freud, not just at the end of the analysis but by persistently denying his interpretations (Freud, 1905a: 58), Freud shows a similar dislike of his young patient. He nearly dismisses the case outright and points out that 'more interesting cases of hysteria have no doubt been published' (Freud, 1905a: 24). Behind that rather flat, impersonal statement lies the fact that he finds her boring. Elsewhere, he is blunt in his judgement: Dora's complaints about her father have 'a wearisome monotony' (Freud, 1905a: 46). This seems harsh, given the circumstances: a father has offered his daughter as a sexual partner to his lover's husband. In light of that shocking fact, Dora's repeated complaints seem more than justified.

Charles Bernheimer makes sense of Freud's dislike through another psychoanalytic concept. Bernheimer argues that it suggests 'a powerfully ambivalent counter-transference'. If 'transference' relates to the projections made by the patient on to the person of the analyst, 'counter-transference' defines the projections made by the analyst on to the patient. Bernheimer argues that Dora's apparent bisexuality, made evident in the feelings for Frau K that Freud so resolutely ignores, confronts Freud with the unresolved homoerotic components of his relationship with his estranged friend Wilhelm Fliess. We are back to the centrality of the relationship between analyst and patient. This is never one-sided. Just as the unresolved desires of the patient are brought to the fore in the analytic setting, so the analyst's own unresolved issues can be played out in the analysis.

This suggests something of the complexity of analytic therapy. Significantly, the room where analysis takes place is not always a place where analyst and patient can meet and form an alliance that makes treatment possible. It can, just as easily, be a place defined by conflict between the two parties.

Despite recognizing the possibility of conflict, little reference is made in these early theoretical reflections to the kind of negative or hostile transference that shaped Dora's case. Freud notes that this phenomenon 'deserves a detailed examination' (Freud, 1912: 106) but does not undertake it. James Strachey, the editor of the *Standard Edition* of Freud's work, comments that, while noting the possibility of a negative transference, 'it is hard to find any other explicit discussions of the subject in Freud's published works' (Freud, 1915a: 161a).

This seems strange. After all, the idea of conflict comes to determine other aspects of Freud's later thought, notably when he formulates the idea of a cosmic battle between Eros and Death. Yet he has little desire to engage with the hostile form the transference takes in the bruising battle with Dora's unconscious. This is what makes her case so interesting. She informs Freud's theory, but at a distance; this distance is necessary if the issues she raises are to be dealt with safely. To deal with Dora's ghost may be troubling; while it is undoubtedly less problematic than confronting an angry, hurt, and betrayed sixteen-year-old, there is still a sense that Freud is not entirely comfortable with the phenomena he encountered in that analysis.

Hysteria and the human animal

Freud's experience of working with hysterics – both good and bad – helps develop his burgeoning theories on clinical practice, as well as his investigation of the powerful psychic forces encountered in the analytic setting. Yet the hysteric also holds a key place in Freud's more general account of what it is to be human.

The processes that determine the way in which the hysteric engages with her world reveal much about how all human beings – not just those who are ill – adapt to their environment. The hysteric holds an important place in Freud's broader speculations about what it is to be human. Freud may be a physician committed to bringing individuals to health but that does not mean that he sees mental illness as somehow detached from the wider context of the activities that make us human. If anything, he seeks to disturb any straightforward distinction between 'normal' and 'abnormal' behaviour. As he puts it, 'every normal person, in fact, is only normal on the average. His ego approximates to that of the psychotic in some part or other and to a greater or lesser extent' (Freud, 1937a: 235). Entering the world of the hysteric enables investigation of the different strategies humans adopt for constructing their world. The extremes of the hysteric's experience – revealed in the symptoms that suggest the attempt to control and regulate their environment – are replicated, to a lesser extent, in the patterns and struggles that determine ordinary human experience.

In his reflections on hysteria and its different historical and cultural manifestations, the contemporary psychoanalyst Christopher Bollas notes that:

> In so many ways – enervation in the nineteenth century, fatigue in the twentieth century – hysterics indicate trouble with the body. It imposes the unwanted and the response to the body's invasion of the self varies from irritated indifference to paranoid grudge.

Because human experience is not just embodied but also involves the ability to reflect, the body can be experienced as something alien to the self. And it is not just the hysteric who experiences 'trouble with the body': many people who manage to function reasonably well in the world also experience problems of distorted self-image, or the fear of death or disease, or the sense that the physical world is not a comfortable place to inhabit. The 'sickness' of the hysteric cannot be completely divorced from the ordinary preoccupations of apparently healthy human beings.

If we broaden this discussion to include a range of neurotic behaviours that bear some relationship to apparently 'normal' motivations and preoccupations, we get a better sense of this connection. In obsessional neurosis (Freud's term for what we now call 'obsessive-compulsive disorder'), the desire to control the unruliness of the external world through self-imposed rituals enables the sufferer to feel safe. But before we write off the sufferer as 'mad' or 'disordered', we might note that the desire to feel safe is reflected in the widespread need for lucky objects or superstitious behaviours such as touching wood. The question of how to feel safe in the world is important for the ill and the healthy, for those who can function in the world and for those who cannot.

That is not to say, of course, that the hysteric or the obsessional neurotic can be understood in exactly the same way as someone who is functioning well in the world. Clearly that presses the point too far. The fact that Freud's patients are not able to live full lives is the main reason that brings them to his consulting room. Freud's concern when he works with them is that of the physician: how to bring about some kind of cure. But it is worth considering how he expresses this aim. He seeks to help them turn their 'hysterical misery into common unhappiness' (Breuer and Freud, 1893–95: 305). This is a fascinating comment, to which we will return later.

Consider the connection between those two words: 'misery' and 'unhappiness'. The first is a more extreme version of the latter but it is connected to Freud's general view of what it is to be human. The human animal can never be entirely happy or satisfied. All that we can hope for is the common or garden dissatisfaction that describes the common lot of humanity. As Thoreau famously commented, 'all men live lives of quiet desperation'. Freud's clinical work lends some weight to this rather bleak analysis.

We might not like this idea, however, so let's pursue it a little longer. The human animal is never satisfied, because unlike its animal relatives it is not at home in its environment. Human society is based on the need to live in communities, to survive the hostility of the world in which we find ourselves. The isolated individual could not survive in such a world. But the protection of society comes at a price: the instinctual drives of sex and aggression must be sublimated and controlled if we are to live together. Civilization offers much but we also lose these base and basic freedoms. Desire cannot always be expressed freely. The human animal has therefore to engage with the stresses and discontents of that restriction.

The repression of basic desires is a fundamental feature of Freud's account of mental processes. The unconscious is the repository of those repressions. In hysteria, inadequate solutions to the problems of sexual desire and the threat felt to the self from 'the unacceptable thought' define symptom formation.

But the distinction between the hysteric and other people is one of degree. The non-hysteric has come up with other, more or less adequate, ways of dealing with their desires that enable them to live in the world. They may, for example, have sublimated such feelings into creativity, religiosity, or philosophy (Freud, 1930: 78–85). But all of us have to deal with our desires and the unruliness that comes with them. To be human is to struggle with finding appropriate ways of balancing our desires with the demands of living in society.

The sublimation of desire into creativity is particularly important for thinking about the way in which the unhappiness of the human condition might be to some extent overcome or, at the very least, made manageable. It also provides another connection between the hysteric's experience and other human activities. The case studies reveal the role that phantasy plays in the life of the hysteric. Anna O refers to her 'private theatre', a world of daydreams that, at times, occupies her completely (Breuer and Freud, 1893–5: 22).

The relationship between phantasy and reality is a complex one in psychoanalytic thought. In *Formulations on the Two Principles of Mental Functioning* (1911), Freud argues that the most basic mental function relates to the unconscious and to the phantasies that babies create when first encountering the external world. Freud tends to see these initial phantasies as attempts at maximizing pleasure. He suggests that the child hallucinates the presence of the absent breast (evidenced through the motion of sucking when the breast is withdrawn) to limit the pain of the absent mother (Freud, 1911: 219 note 4). Such hallucinations, however, do not bring satisfaction and it is this disappointment that contributes to the development of a second mental principle concerned with reality: phantasies need to be checked against the experience of the external world.

Clearly, it would be a mistake to live just in the world of phantasy. Freud notes that 'if phantasies become over-luxuriant

and over-powerful, the conditions are laid for an onset of neurosis
or psychosis' (Freud, 1908a [1907]: 148). This is clearly so in Anna
O's case. But he is also aware that such phantasies – playing with
ideas in imagination – are common to all: 'most people construct
phantasies at times in their lives' (Freud, 1908a [1907]: 145). More
than that, it is the willingness to engage with our phantasies that
forms the basis of human artistic creativity.

When Freud addresses the sources of creativity, he connects
the creative writer to the lost world of childhood. The creative
writer is like the child at play: the writer 'creates a world of phantasy which he takes very seriously – that is, which he invests with
large amounts of emotion' (Freud, 1908a [1907]: 144). Freud
drives home this connection: 'every child at play behaves like a
creative writer, in that he creates a world of his own or, rather,
re-arranges the things of his world in a new way which pleases
him' (Freud, 1908a [1907]: 143–4). One is reminded of the powerful pull of the phantastical world for the hysteric, although
whether it 'pleases her' in quite the same way is not immediately
obvious. What these different perspectives suggest is a similar
desire to shape the world according to one's will. In all these
cases, what is being attempted is the construction of a vision of
reality; a vision that makes the individual feel secure in a threatening and unpredictable universe. There is, then, a link between
the creativity of the hysteric who is trying to find a way of
making sense of her world and her desires and the strategies that
someone who is not suffering from hysteria applies to construct
their own life. The human animal is able to construct things of
real beauty and in the phantasies of the hysteric – played out on
her body – a similarly creative process is at work. The continuum
between health and sickness is one with which Freud is willing
to work. As he develops his account of humanity, he is particularly
concerned to consider what can be learnt from those struggling
to make sense of their feelings and lives.

Connecting the thought-processes of the 'sick' and the 'healthy' is particularly important when considering Freud's theory of sexuality. As we have seen, the 'solution' of Dora's case, for Freud, involved highlighting her desire to take the place of both her mother and Frau K in her father's affections. If we accept Freud's conclusions, we might see such a desire as highlighting the extent of Dora's illness. But Freud is not prepared to see such apparently perverse phantasies and incestuous desires as simply a feature of hysteria and thus something derived from sickness. Instead, he suggests that these unconscious desires are universal. As a result, he places the Oedipus complex at the heart of his theory of human sexuality.

3
Oedipus and sexuality

The figure of the hysteric is at the heart of Freud's development of psychoanalysis. His theory – both of mental illness and what it is to be human – is shaped by what emerges from those therapeutic conversations. And just as the hysteric is vital for understanding the development of his ideas, so his account of sexuality cannot be understood without reference to the figure of Oedipus.

Freud's use of a fictional character to shape his theory says much about how he understands the nature of sexual development. Sexuality is dynamic. It does not emerge ready-made. It is not merely linked to what we might think of as the pull of instinctual life. Human sexuality is shaped through a series of stages, each of which Freud connects with the experience of pleasure. It begins with the pleasure of sucking (the oral stage), then moves to the holding and releasing of faeces (the anal stage), before arriving at the experiences connected with the genitals (the phallic stage). Each of these stages leads the individual from childhood into adulthood but none of them can be understood simply in terms of bodily processes. Freud's theory is a psycho-sexual one; this means that sexual experiences are not reducible to bodily sensations but are accompanied by powerful fantasies. Under the forces of repression, our early imaginings may have been expelled from the mind, and apparently forgotten, but they continue to play a powerful role in how we live our lives.

We see this in Freud's depiction of two ways in which desire can be structured. We might follow what he calls 'the anaclitic' model for desire. This means that our love objects represent those on whom we depended as children. Or we might follow the 'narcissistic' model for desire. In this model, our love objects resemble our image of ourselves. Whatever path we take, the shaping of sexuality involves the repetition of our individual histories of love and development. Animal instincts are not the only factor in the course of sexuality.

Against this backdrop, Freud's use of an ancient story plays itself out. The story he chooses to shape and illustrate his theory is a disturbing one, drawn from Ancient Greek drama. In Sophocles's play, *Oedipus Rex*, Oedipus has unwittingly married his mother and killed his father. A disturbing idea, to say the least; one that Freud renders even more disturbing. Rather than see Oedipus' fate as a horrifying – and individual – aberration, he sees it as expressing the long-forgotten desires of childhood that accompany and shape every individual's sexual development. Between the ages of three and five, every child must struggle with what comes to be called 'the Oedipus complex', when, like the Greek king, they long to be rid of the parent of the same sex in order to take possession of the parent of the opposite sex.

This claim remains controversial. Freud accepted that for many it would render psychoanalysis unacceptable (Freud, 1905b: 226n). The complex informs and shapes another similarly startling claim: children are sexual beings. We should be careful how we interpret this notion, as it must always be read against Freud's contention that sex is never just about genital acts but also about the imagination. In Freud's hands, the story of Oedipus becomes a powerful – and adaptable – way of exploring and mapping the development of human sexuality.

Freud and Oedipus

Why does Freud attach his account of sexuality to Oedipus' story? Using a piece of drama seems to fly in the face of the scientific grounding he wishes to provide for his nascent theory. But as he seeks to map the idea of the unconscious, he is aware of just how difficult it is to provide empirical evidence for unconscious processes. By its very nature, the unconscious cannot be accessed directly. We only see it as through a glass darkly; the methods for understanding forces driven from consciousness are of necessity going to be rather different from the methods employed by empirical science.

When Freud uses Oedipus, he draws attention to the continuing power of this tale. It is a story of horror, blood, violence, and incest. It has a shocking conclusion, for when Oedipus discovers what he has done, he puts out his eyes. The sheer repellence of the tale should make watching it almost impossible, yet over its two-thousand-year history it has been consistently performed. Freud is interested in determining what drives the continuing fascination with Oedipus. His answer is simple. The story fascinates because it speaks directly to each one of us:

> The Greek legend seizes on a compulsion which everyone recognizes because he feels its existence within himself. Each member of the audience was once, in germ and in phantasy, just such an Oedipus and each one recoils in horror from the dream-fulfilment here transplanted into reality, with the whole quota of repression which separates his infantile state from his present one (Freud, 1897: 265).

Freud's highly contentious claim is that we have all shared Oedipus' murderous and sexual desires. The peculiar mixture of repulsion and fascination felt on encountering this story signifies what Freud calls the 'return of the repressed' (Freud, 1919: 249). The play is powerful because it reawakens desires that we have long since forgotten and that we would rather remained forgotten. In the drama, we can safely experience the desires of our early years; desires which reflect our earliest relationships with our parents.

At the heart of the Oedipus story are what Freud sees as the common incestuous desires of childhood. He suggests that the prohibitions against incest in all cultures only make sense if this apparently repellent act is something that, at one time, we all wanted to do. If we had not desired it, we would have no need to prohibit it.

Freud first mentions Oedipus in a letter to his close friend Wilhelm Fliess, written on 15 October 1897, some time after the publication of the *Studies on Hysteria*. Freud is in the midst of his self-analysis. If the *Studies* reveal the difficult family relationships and unacceptable desires (often involving a parent) that led to the illnesses of his neurotics, Freud notes that this self-investigation has led him to identify similar desires:

> To be completely honest with oneself is good practice. One single thought of general value has been revealed to me. I have found, in my case too, falling in love with the mother and jealousy of the father and I now regard it as a universal event of early childhood (Freud, 1897: 265).

While Freud does not use the idea of a 'complex' at this stage, he is keen to claim that these feelings do not result from some quirk in his character. He wants to move from the idea that it reflects his psyche to seeing such feelings as a universal feature of human development. This is quite a leap; clearly Freud will have to provide evidence to support such a move if his readers are to agree with him.

In his first full discussion of the Oedipus complex, in *The Interpretation of Dreams* (1900), Freud attempts to provide evidence by drawing attention to dreams about the death of the parent of the same sex. At this point in his discussion, he has claimed that all dreams can be read as expressing the wishes of the dreamer. In the dream, wishes are fulfilled (Freud, 1900: 122–33). Read thus, death-dreams are extremely shocking, for they suggest that at one time or another we desired the death of the parent whose sex we share: a wish that the dream is realizing.

Freud goes further: such dreams express not just hostility but also the child's early sexual preference. At this stage, he formulates the complex in fairly simple terms: desire for the parent of the opposite sex; hostility towards the parent of the same sex. Later, a more complex theory emerges, which allows a range of attitudes to develop towards one's parents, to be experienced and then to be replaced. At this point, however, Freud is working out the key mechanisms of the complex. Death-dreams provide examples, he claims, of the rivalry and desire that shapes the child's relationship with its parents. It is 'as though boys regarded their fathers and girls their mothers as their rivals in love, whose elimination could not fail to be to their advantage' (Freud, 1900: 256). 'The advantage' lies in taking the place of the parent who has been eliminated, just as in the story of Oedipus, killing his father, Laius, enables Oedipus to marry – albeit unbeknown to him – his mother, Jocasta.

Children harbouring such murderous desires sounds far-fetched. Not only that, it flies in the face of the deepest-held beliefs about the innocence of children. Freud accepts there will be resistance to such unpalatable ideas and attempts to persuade the reader by providing more evidence. If we are doubtful that children feel as he suggests, he asks us to listen to what they say:

> A particularly gifted and lively girl of four, in whom this piece of child psychology is especially transparent, declared quite openly: 'Mummy can go away now. Then Daddy must marry me and I'll be his wife'. Such a wish in a child is not the least inconsistent with her being tenderly attached to her mother (Freud, 1900: 258).

Freud quickly explains what the desire for death means in this context. It is the absence of the parent of the same sex that is desired, which would then enable the child to take the place of the parent. Death, for children, is associated with absence rather than annihilation. But, as Freud notes, the effect is the same: '"dead" people … are always away and never come back' (Freud, 1900: 258).

We may remain unconvinced by such anecdotal evidence. It is haphazard; far from methodical. More than that, it is one thing to say children aspire to adult life – and in the nuclear families of western society, marriage may well be seen as a key marker of this adult experience – but quite another to claim that they sexually desire their parent. Freud will not be put off; he pushes on, drawing on clinical material derived from his patients' experiences. Freud claimed that many of his patients said that they had been seduced as children, often by a parent. Initially, he takes these claims at face value but as he develops his theory he becomes less convinced: not least because if true, it would seem that there is an epidemic of child sexual abuse. Rather than accept this notion, he claims that these desires express primarily psychic experiences, not empirical realities.

While Freud connects the phantasy of seduction with neurotic illness, he does not claim that only neurotics have these desires. We all experience similar desires. Freud wishes to draw our attention to the way in which sexual instincts are played out both on the body and in the mental realm. The energy associated with sexual desire – libido – has to be expressed in some way. The difference between the apparently healthy person and the neurotic is that the neurotic's illness emanates from their inability adequately to resolve the tensions and wishes that define their desires. We have seen something of what this means in the lives of the hysterics. What happens if the desires of the Oedipal complex are not resolved? What happens if the child has not adequately detached his desires from 'his' parents in order to become a part of the wider social community? If such a failure occurs:

> The son remains all his life bowed beneath his father's authority
> … unable to transfer his libido to an outside sexual object.

> With the relationship changed round, the same fate can await
> the daughter. In this sense, the Oedipus complex may justly be
> regarded as the nucleus of the neuroses (Freud, 1916–17: 337).

Freud believes that he has found a good example of this possibility
in a patient known as 'the Rat Man' (identified by many commentators as Ernst Lanzer). Freud claims that the Rat Man's
inability to accept his murderous feelings towards his father
determines the shape of his illness. To ease his feelings of anxiety,
he has instigated a number of rituals that have to be enacted. This
'obsessional neurosis' has limited his ability to act in the world.
He is stuck; unable to live in a fulfilling way.

At the heart of this debilitating illness, Freud identifies an
'unacceptable' thought the Rat Man had when he first experienced sexual intercourse: 'This is glorious! One might murder
one's father for this!'(Freud, 1909b: 201). Rather than confront
the ambivalent feelings this thought reveals about his father, he
has sought to bury it. The consequence is that he now fears what
may befall his father and family at the hands of a hostile world and
has constructed a series of rituals to manage those fears. (The all-
consuming fear that grips him, and that gives him his pseudonym,
involves a legendary Chinese torture technique, which he
believes will befall his loved ones if he fails to act in this highly
regulated and ritualized way. In this torture, a pot containing rats
is strapped to the victim's buttocks. To escape, the rats must gnaw
their way out through the victim's anus.) Behind this view of the
world as a hostile place lies the Rat Man's inability to own and
accept his unacknowledged feelings of hatred towards his father.
Projected outwards, these feelings come to distort his view of the
world in a way that makes living his life impossible.

If an inadequate resolution of the complex lies at the root of
neurotic illness – and we shall have much more to discuss in a
moment about the 'resolution' of the complex – Freud does not
want his reader to focus too much on the experience of the neurotic.

He does not want the complex to be understood primarily as a feature of the life-experience of the mentally ill. Its resolution is, rather, a task everyone has to face (Freud, 1916–17: 337).

Whether we are prepared to accept Freud's theory largely depends on our response to the story of Oedipus. Is it as fascinating and repelling to us as it was to Freud? If we rigorously investigate our childhood memories, do we find evidence to support his claim that at one time we wanted to take the place of the parent of the same sex? Such support – if we find it – is by nature subjective. This makes the basis for accepting the complex rather weak. Indeed, much of Freud's argument depends on 'evidence' gleaned from his self-analysis. At the same time, he draws on the experiences of his patients who are suffering from various forms of mental illness. Such sources seem far from compelling, particularly if Freud wishes us to see the complex as a universal feature of human life.

An early criticism, made by the anthropologist Bronislaw Malinowski, highlights the problems of making the shift from the complex as something individual to something universal. Malinowski argues that the most one can say of the complex is that it might emerge from a particular way of organising relationships at a particular time in western history. It reflects the structures of the nuclear family but cannot be applied to societies that structure society and family life rather differently. Freud's problem is that he wants it to be universal when there is no evidence that it is.

Malinowski's comments suggest that the theory will inevitably be rather limited in scope. But perhaps this criticism ignores how Freud uses Oedipus' story. At times he stretches the application and interpretation of the story almost to breaking point; this suggests that it is less a means of denoting a particular set of evidenced theories than a creative driver of his thinking. It underpins not only his distinctive account of individual sexual development but also the forces that shape human social structures.

The changing shape of the Oedipus complex

When Freud describes human sexuality, he does so against the backdrop of the child's earliest relationships. Our desires and fears concerning our parents in the first few years of life determine our character and our relationships. Sex, as such, is never something that happens only between two people, because we carry these desires and fears – albeit unconsciously – into our adult relationships. There are always six people in the room when we have sex: the couple and both sets of parents.

Taking a story as emblematic of this shifting experience provides a flexible way of engaging with the psychical experience of sex. Sex involves physical acts that take place against the backdrop of the phantasies that each partner has about these acts; phantasies forged by their earliest experiences of their parents. Just as stories can be read differently, different parts of the story capturing our imagination on different occasions, so at different points in the development of Freud's theory of sexuality, different ways of formulating Oedipus' story come to the fore. Nowhere is this more evident than when Freud turns his attention to female sexual development.

Freud's discussion of female sexuality unfolds as he addresses the question of how the complex is resolved. How do we move from childhood desire into the world of adult sexual relations? Initially, Freud assumes that an account of the infant's sexuality can ignore the gendered nature of human beings. As so often, male theorists ignore female experience and make a straightforward identification between 'man' and 'the human'. Freud is no different: when he details the twists and turns of the complex, which have to be negotiated from childhood to adulthood, he does so primarily through discussion of the boy's complex. Once he has mapped these changing attachments, he then applies his theory (rather clumsily) to girls (Freud, 1916–17: 333).

The Oedipus complex unfolds against his model of staged sexual development. Because sexual development involves stages, the outcome of this process is never certain. There is always the possibility of disruption: phases overlap and it is possible that an individual might get stuck in a stage that influences their later choice of sexual object or practice. I might, for example, remain committed to the pleasures of sucking that denote the oral stage, and limit my sexual experiences to oral sex rather than genital intercourse. Tracking sexual development in this way suggests that the ultimate aim of sexual development is reproduction, an assumption that apparently contradicts Freud's expansion of the concept of human sexuality to involve so much more than genital activity. This is the tension that runs beneath his account of the Oedipus complex as it shifts and develops.

How does Freud understand the boy's complex and what problems does this throw up when he tries to relate the male experience to that of the female? The Oedipus complex emerges during the phallic stage of development. At this time, the pleasures of masturbation are being explored most fully. During this stage, the boy thinks that all individuals have a penis that enchants them in the same way his penis enchants him. And when he thinks all individuals have a penis he really does mean 'all': both males and females (Freud, 1923b: 141–5). Eventually, the boy comes to realize that this isn't so. Through play, or bath-time, or accident, he discovers that some individuals do not have penises. This comes as a shock. In trying to make sense of this lack, he arrives at the conclusion that these individuals have been castrated. And if they have had their penises removed, presumably there is no reason why such a fate should not also befall him.

The question then arises as to who has the power to castrate? The boy looks around for a suitable contender for this task and fixes on the father (a choice, it should be noted, that reflects the patriarchal structure of the family of Freud's time and class). The boy's fears of castration are probably linked to threats associated with his adventures in masturbation: 'If you keep fiddling with that it'll drop off.' He thinks that the father knows of his desires for the mother. Fearful, guilty, and ashamed, he represses these desires. This is an important point to reach, for in repressing his desires, the agency for morality – the superego – is formed. The complex is repressed or destroyed (though in practice it is never completely eradicated). This sounds like a sorry tale of lost plea-sure and the arrival of guilt. But all is not lost: the hope remains that one day he will attain the power that accompanies possession of the penis when he reaches adulthood and takes on the mantle of his father.

When it comes to the girl's experience, at first Freud simply reverses the process (Freud, 1916–17: 333): the girl desires her father while seeing her mother as her rival. This is not particu-larly satisfactory; as late as 1923 Freud is giving an excuse for the tensions in his theory that has the power to drive grown women to distraction. He suggests the process of sexual development in girls is ultimately mysterious; it remains 'not known to us' (Freud, 1923b: 142). This is not a very satisfactory response. As the con-temporary psychoanalyst Luce Irigaray says, in commenting on similar statements by Lacan about the 'mysterious' nature of female sexuality, why not ask women themselves about their experiences? That might easily dispel the idea that female experi-ence is mysterious and unknowable. Indeed, Freud comes under pressure to revise his theory from early women analysts such as Karen Horney, who attempt to define these supposedly 'unknown' experiences. Pushed in this way, he comes to formulate an account of the girl's Oedipus complex that is more convoluted than the boy's, involving a different sequence of events and stages, which suggests that female sexuality is clearly not as 'mysterious' as Freud first thought.

How does Freud define the girl's Oedipus complex? Interest-ingly, his focus shifts to the period before its onset. This earlier period is not dwelt upon in the same way when he describes the boy's experience. In boys, the mother is the first love-object and remains so during the complex and throughout the boy's life.

Things are rather different for the girl: at first, the mother is her love-object but their relationship is more complex, because to become a woman the girl must 'change her erotogenic zone and her object' (Freud, 1933: 119). In other words, if the girl is to attain 'true' womanhood, she must move from a sexuality shaped by female relationships to one shaped by relationships with men. This necessitates making the shift from pleasure sited in the clitoris to pleasure located in the vagina and, significantly, from identifying with the mother – her first love-object – to the father who will provide the model for her future relationships with men. With good reason, feminists have responded angrily to such an idea. Not only does it ignore – as Anne Koedt famously notes – the biological fact that female sexual pleasure is primarily located in the clitoris, it also assumes that to be happy and fulfilled, women need men.

As he describes the relationship between the girl and her mother, Freud focuses on the experience of ambivalence. Love and hostility towards the mother unite in the girl in a way that is not so evident from considering the boy's experience. The girl's early sexual wishes during the phallic phase are either to impregnate the mother or to bear her a child. This mother Freud describes as 'the *phallic* mother' (Freud, 1933: 126), endowed in the child's imagination with a penis just like the father's. When the girl discovers that her mother does not possess a penis, her attachment to the mother 'ends in hate' (Freud, 1933: 121). The girl's attachment now shifts to the father.

At the heart of this movement is the castration complex. Not only is the mother without a penis but 'girls hold their mother responsible for their lack of a penis and do not forgive her for their being put at a disadvantage' (Freud, 1933: 124). Recognizing that not only is her mother 'castrated' *but so is she* is a turning point for the girl's sexuality and her choice of objects. In recognizing her status as castrated, the girl can respond in one of three ways. She can either become sexually inhibited or neurotic, or she can seek to acquire a penis through pursuing masculine goals. Alternatively, she can follow the path to what Freud defines as 'normal' femininity, whereby a man is seen as the possessor of the penis the girl wants and can get either through possessing him or through producing with him a child who will become the penis for her. In this latter course, the father becomes of crucial importance, for it is through the father that the girl initially hopes to have the child who will be her 'penis substitute' (see Freud, 1933: 128). Thus the wish for a baby with her father heralds the start of the girl's Oedipus complex.

No wonder feminists are angered by Freud's theory! But let us put aside our sense of outrage for a moment and consider what this more convoluted process of female sexual development might tell us both about the changing shape of Freud's theory and Freud as a theorist.

As his theory develops, sexual development is no longer understood as the same for male and female. The Oedipus complex in girls is 'the outcome of a long and difficult development' (Freud, 1933: 129) involving shifting and ambivalent feelings for her mother. While for the boy the threat of castration destroys his Oedipal desires, for the girl 'the castration complex *prepares* for the Oedipus complex' (Freud, 1933: 129; my emphasis). Freud goes further. When the Oedipus complex arrives, it is for the girl 'a haven of refuge' (Freud, 1933: 129) after the trials and tribulations of her early identifications. Because she does not experience the threat of castration – she is, after all, already castrated in her own mind – she can stay at the stage of desiring the father's child for 'an indeterminate length of time' (Freud, 1933: 129). Eventually, she realizes that the father will not give her the child she desires and so the complex is dissolved, ending with her feeling disappointed with her father and renewing her attachment to her mother. Freud argues that the complex in the girl is demolished late and 'incompletely' (Freud, 1933: 129), an eventuality that ultimately affects the kind of relationships women will have with the men who come to take the place of the father. If the girl fails to accept that she is castrated she develops 'a masculinity complex' and may seek homosexual relationships.

Such is the story that Freud presents. Whatever we might think of it – and it may well leave us hooting with derision – considering the shifting detail of his theory suggests something of its adaptability. It is not a rigid account that cannot be modified when new ideas come to light. If we want contemporary evidence, we might consider Juliet Mitchell's adaptation of the theory to address sibling relationships. At the same time, the development of the theory reveals how Freud works as a theorist. His account of the complex develops over a period of some thirty-six years, during which time he adapts and changes it as criticisms are made and new ideas come to the fore. Freud is often criticised for simply adapting female experience to fit a pre-formed male model but this is largely incorrect. This might hold true of his early comments but the later theory is concerned with paying attention to the distinctive experience of the girl.

That is not to say, of course, that the theory is unproblematic for understanding what it is to be a woman. The central, determining role ascribed to the penis – having it or lacking it – suggests that Freud's theories arise primarily from his reflections on his male experience. The male body is taken as the 'normal' (or normative) body for understanding human experience. This is perhaps not surprising, given the central role of a male protagonist in the story that is used to illuminate it. The girl's developing sexuality is theorized against an assumption that she will envy the boy for possessing a penis and that she will assume that she is somehow lacking – that she is castrated. But why should she? Why shouldn't she assume the boy is deformed, lacking her bodily integrity and hampered by a vulnerable flap of skin?

Other evidence from Freud's case studies suggests in similar fashion a rather different way of considering envy in childhood. Little Hans was fascinated by his mother's ability to give birth and phantasized about giving birth to a little girl (Freud, 1909a: 87). Similarly, one of Melanie Klein's later case studies describes her child patient, Richard's, fascination with producing babies. This leads her to claim that envy of the mother's ability to produce babies is significant for the child's developing psyche. This suggests a particular weakness with defining the complex against the backdrop of Freud's fascination with a male hero. The role of the father becomes overly important and what might be called 'womb-envy' is ignored for an account of the kind of identifications that might shape the child's experience.

As it is, the implications of Freud's theory for women are far from positive, most importantly in terms of the moral life. Freud locates the development of morality and conscience in the sphere of the superego. The superego is created out of the resolution of the Oedipus complex and becomes the internalized voice of parental prohibitions and societal demands. Because women feel no fear of castration, as they are castrated already, they do not experience the fear of punishment which provides the basis for moral action. Women emerge as 'less moral' than men (Freud, 1925b).

Female identity, through Freud's lens, takes on a tragic note. While both the boy and girl are faced with loss when it comes to the end (or 'dissolution') of the complex, the girl's position is decidedly more perilous than that of the boy. The girl's experience involves the loss of her own (and her sex's) sense of power, as well as the loss of her father. At least the boy is able to emerge from the reign of the complex with the hope that he will eventually take his father's place in securing his own family and becoming its head.

That this notion of moral development flies in the face of experience challenges the moral implications that Freud claims.

'The greater moral conscience of the male' is not translated into action, the majority of crimes being committed by men. The unconscious fear of punishment does not seem to make much difference to how men behave.

Before we decide that the theory is broken beyond repair, we might consider an alternative perspective. According to Lou Andreas-Salomé, woman is 'the fortunate animal' whose adaptation to her environment is more successful than the male's. Unlike the male, who must seek his fulfilment in the attempt to overcome and surpass the father, woman's happiness is grounded in an altogether more secure sense of who she is. Far from being 'immoral', there is a close connection between woman and the cycles of the natural world which so trouble Freud's conflicted human being. Woman, because of her complex sexual development, is happier, ultimately, than the male. Because she returns to the mother, her selfhood is unified and grounded in a way that his is not.

Assessing the Oedipus complex

Innovative as Andreas-Salomé's reading may be, it depends on accepting a view of woman as different from the male. She is more passive and less active than he is. While feminists like Luce Irigaray have similarly pursued ideas of sexual difference, others have challenged the effect that prioritising Oedipus has had upon the shape of psychoanalytic theory. At one level, it simply reworks the old, dismissive accounts in the Western philosophical tradition of 'Woman' as emotional, passive, and lacking reason and morality. All that differs is the attempt to verse such ideas in 'scientific' language. More generally, it is difficult to see what solid evidence can be provided for the existence of the complex. Its power is dependent on the extent to which Freud's reader is prepared to accept the reality of the experiences that lead Freud to postulate it in the first place.

Emphasising the subjective dimension gives rise to the most damaging criticism. The evidence Freud provides to establish the existence of the complex can be read rather differently if one challenges the primacy he gives the complex to shape the experiences under discussion. The case study of Little Hans provides a fine example. Here, Freud reflects upon – largely at second-hand – the analysis of a five-year-old boy by his father (Freud, 1909a). As R. D. Hinshelwood argues, this analysis is problematic, not least because the boy's father (a committed follower of Freud) does not appear to listen to what his son says but spends his time pursuing those aspects of the case which seem to confirm key aspects of Freudian theory. This raises an interesting question. Does Freud's reliance on the Oedipus complex as an interpretative tool force material into a shape that coheres with it, rather than letting the material speak for itself?

Hans's dream of the giraffes provides a telling case in point. In this dream, Hans tells of seeing two giraffes – one big, one crumpled – in his room. The big one calls out, while Hans sits on the crumpled one (Freud, 1909a: 37–40). His father interprets this dream as expressing his desire to take possession of his mother, thus making the dream conform to the pattern of the Oedipus complex (Freud, 1909a: 41). Hinshelwood suggests an alternative interpretation, focusing on the pressures facing a child being questioned in such an intrusive way by his father. For Hinshelwood, Hans's dream reveals the child's hostility to his father's attempt to interpret and scrutinize his behaviour.

Later analysts have also been hampered by Freud's model. When Ruth Mack Brunswick becomes analyst to the Wolf Man some years after his analysis with Freud, she identifies the attachment of her patient to the sister who seduced him as a child. However, she largely ignores this in her discussion of his illness. Instead, she prefers to focus on 'a remnant of the transference to Freud' and thus the Wolf Man's apparent 'father-fixation'. A similar omission, as we have seen, occurs in Freud's analysis of Dora.

Emphasising the roles of her father and Herr K means that discussion of Dora's relationships with women is alluded to in passing but not addressed in much detail.

While Freud reads the Oedipus story primarily through the relationship of father and son, father and daughter, it needn't be read in this way. This is perhaps the point that opens up the possibilities inherent in the story of Oedipus. For the analysts who come after Freud, it is the flexibility possible in the framework it provides for understanding the desires that accompany sexual development that makes it useful.

Consider Melanie Klein's account of the complex. For Klein, the complex arises between the ages of two and three-quarters and four: considerably earlier than Freud's dating, at around the age of five. Klein argues that genital desires are directed towards both parents and that the child is aware of both the penis and the vagina. More importantly, she shifts from talk of 'the Oedipus complex' to 'the Oedipal situation'. This change of terminology emphasizes the need for the child to acknowledge the parents' relationship. The parents have a relationship that excludes the child, which opens up the importance of a 'third position' for the child's developing sense of relationship with others. Julia Kristeva extends this idea, placing the complex in the context of the shift that the child must make from the symbiotic connection with the mother to the acceptance that there are others outside that relationship. Making this shift is necessary if the child is to relate to others. The father is significant, as his presence disrupts any overly cloying relationship between mother and child, thus allowing the space for relationship, language, and the possibility of love to develop.

Such interpretations suggest considerable flexibility in the Oedipus story. It does not have to be read in a restrictive way. This raises questions about the kind of discipline psychoanalysis is. It could be understood to offer a scientific hypothesis about the nature of human being, a view that clearly Freud espoused.

But the evidence for the Oedipus complex is not that strong, largely because it is grounded in an account of unconscious processes that may or may not be accepted by the reader. Before we give up on psychoanalysis and find something better to do, we could think of psychoanalysis differently. We could think of it as a method that provides a way of exploring one's life which is more akin to the creative processes that go into the writing of a story.

Such an account of psychoanalysis informs Bruno Bettelheim's work. Bettelheim claims that too much emphasis has been placed upon viewing psychoanalysis as a science at the expense of considering the way Freud uses his knowledge of classical literature and everyday experiences to formulate his key theories. Bettelheim argues that Freud uses the term 'Oedipus complex' as a metaphor that, in common with all metaphors, is valuable precisely because it is open to a variety of interpretations. To explore these varied interpretations it is necessary to immerse oneself in the myth. He returns to Sophocles's story, showing not only how it relates to the child's development but also how it reveals the ambivalent attitude that the parent has to the child. As he says, we sometimes forget that Jocasta and Laius have tried to murder the child they believe to be capable of destroying them: in Sophocles's play, Jocasta has had Oedipus exposed on a hillside and left to die.

Employing Bettelheim's method opens up a range of new possibilities for using the complex. Freud uses the complex in a hierarchical way, his interest being in the relationships between parent and child. Yet this hierarchical emphasis, while important, is not inevitable, particularly if one returns to Sophocles's cycle of plays concerned with the history of the House of Cadmus. In the third of the Theban plays, *Antigone*, the focus shifts from the fate of Oedipus to that of his children. Antigone's concern with the fate of her brothers suggests that relationships between siblings are as significant for how we understand ourselves as the relationships between parents and children; an approach that Juliet

Mitchell also takes. Seeing the story of Oedipus as an imaginative way of opening up discussion of a range of relationships may be more useful than seeing it as a scientific hypothesis.

Oedipus and human society

If the strength of the evidence for the complex in the area of individual psychosexual development is not particularly strong, we may find ourselves baffled by Freud's attempt to relate the complex to the social realm. Moved from the personal to the social realm, it becomes the bedrock for understanding the origins of religion and, to a large extent, society itself.

This development comes in *Totem and Taboo* (1913), in which Freud examines the role of totemism in so-called 'primitive' forms of religion. In totemism, an animal is given the status of guardian of the tribe, meaning that it cannot be killed or eaten. In attempting to explain this – and the perplexing (apparently contradictory) ritual slaughter of this sacred animal – Freud discerns powerful overlaps with the driving forces of the Oedipus complex. In totemic systems, assent is given to two basic laws: 'not to kill the totem animal and to avoid sexual intercourse with members of the totem clan of the opposite sex' (Freud, 1913a: 32). The dynamic of sex and death exemplified in the story of Oedipus, which structures the development of the individual's Oedipus complex, is reflected in the injunctions that shape and structure the earliest form of human society. Oedipus isn't just relevant for understanding psychosexual processes; his story also informs the structures of human society.

Freud's investigation is primarily interested in exploring the psychical forces that support human social structures and activities. Why the taboos on incest, killing the totem animal and the dead? What do they tell us about the psychic processes supporting such social attitudes? His answer focuses on the ambivalence felt towards the taboo object. It is sacred but it is also "'dangerous'", "unclean", and "uncanny'" (Freud, 1913a: 22). Fear and desire lie behind these beliefs; he identifies these fears and desires with the same emotions that accompany individual development.

How does he do this? Initially, he turns his attention to the significance of the prohibition against incest that is common to all forms of human society. A taboo is only necessary if you want to do what it commands you not to do. Thus, incest must be something that, at some stage, was universally desired. More than that: Freud argues that in the world of the 'primitive', mother-incest is seen as the most problematic and subject to the most taboos. Considering the figure of the mother–in–law, Freud suggests that the strict practices which regulate her relationship with her son–in–law reveal something of the strengths of such desires (Freud, 1913a: 13–14). As mother–in–law, rather than birth-mother, she both masks and reveals the unacceptable desires a man has for his mother. (Think about that next time a dodgy comedian tells a joke about his mother–in–law.)

If the desire for incest is so strong, why the taboo? Why not follow the libertines of the Marquis de Sade's stories and enjoy these desires to the full? Freud's answer comes from identifying the same connection between fear and desire that informed his discussion of Oedipus. The father is feared, the mother desired. In taboo, 'the fear is stronger than the desire' (Freud, 1913a: 31). Why? The answer lies in the totem animal, which he sees as a substitute for the father. His evidence is, in part, based upon evidence drawn from his investigation of childhood phobias. Little Hans suffered from a fear of horses. In analysis, this was linked to fears of the 'castrating father'. The horse who might 'bite' is the father, who could punish Hans's desire that his father might die so that he could have sole access to his mother (see Freud, 1913a: 128–132). At this point, Freud makes a move that seems strange, if not ridiculous, to his critics. The psychical forces he has thus far been at pains to describe and explore are related to an actual killing of a father in pre-history. It is this distant event that continues to exert a power over how we view our own fathers.

Freud comes to the conclusion that there was a first killing of the father through consideration of the totem meal. The totem animal is – against the strictures of the taboo – killed and eaten, amid great festivities. Once eaten, 'the slaughtered animal is lamented and bewailed' (Freud, 1913a: 140). Drawing upon Darwin's theory of a primal horde as the first form of human society, Freud develops a story that explains this ritual and, moreover, the forces that shape human society. He identifies an actual murder to which the ritual meal alludes. Denied sexual access to the women of the tribe by the father who has sole rights over them, his sons 'killed and devoured their father and so made an end of the patriarchal horde' (Freud, 1913a: 141). The ritual meal is a re-enactment of this original cannibalistic killing. Yet the death of the father does not bring the solace and fulfilment for which the brothers hoped:

> They hated their father, who presented such a formidable obstacle to their craving for power and their sexual desires; but they loved and admired him too. After they had got rid of him, had satisfied their hatred and had put into effect their wish to identify themselves with him, the affection which had all this time been pushed under was bound to make itself felt. It did so in the form of remorse. A sense of guilt made its appearance, which in this instance coincided with the remorse felt by the whole group. The dead father became stronger than the living one had been … They revoked their deed by forbidding the killing of the totem, the substitute for the father; and they renounced its fruit by resigning their claim to the women who had now been set free. They thus created out of their filial sense of guilt the two fundamental taboos of totemism, which for that very reason inevitably corresponded to the repressed wishes of the Oedipus complex (Freud, 1913a: 143).

The Oedipus complex thus moves from being an account of the earliest relations between a child and its parents into the realm of history. We are dealing with real events, rather than psychic phantasies. At the same time, these events explain certain psychic processes, for the dead father is feared and desired and his 'return' is experienced in the guilt felt for his murder. This guilt does not stop with his sons but is passed down through the generations.

Not surprisingly, this proposal has been criticised, largely on the grounds that there is little proof for Freud's claims. As the anthropologist E.E. Evans-Pritchard put it, *Totem and Taboo* is no more than a 'just-so story'. Freud recognizes the speculative nature of these reflections and the objections that might well be raised: 'It would be as foolish to aim at exactitude in such questions as it would be unfair to insist upon certainty' (Freud, 1913a: 143 note). However, his reticence should not blind the reader to the use Freud makes of the story as he develops his psychohistory of human culture. The formation of society and the values that drive its continuance are based upon complicity in the father's murder; religion and its rituals are based on a communal sense of guilt and remorse; systems of morality are based upon the tensions between demand and penance (Freud, 1913a: 146). All can be traced back to the killing of the father; all are grounded in this historical expression of the Oedipus complex.

How to interpret this? The philosopher Paul Ricoeur addresses the story's dubious historical basis and argues that it is best understood as a myth. Before we dismiss a myth as something untrue, we should note that it offers much more than a false tale; it is a creative story expressing a profound truth. Freud provides a narrative that makes sense of the Oedipus complex that he has identified in his self-analysis and in his work with his patients. In this story, he is able to relate individual psychosexual development to the forces that constructed the earliest human societies.

Does Ricoeur's rendition help? We have already considered feminist objections to the central role given to the complex for understanding human sexuality – and particularly female sexuality – and it is worth returning to the feminist critique. In *Totem and Taboo*, religion and society are understood through the lens of the relationship between father and sons (Freud, 1913a: 146). Where are mothers and daughters in all this pontificating about the foundations of human cultural life? Are we to assume, with the cultural critic Camille Paglia, that women are largely absent from the processes that shaped human culture? (Paglia argues that if the construction of human society had been left to women, we would still be living in grass huts.) To accept this rendition is to find oneself, with Freud, unable to account for the great mother goddesses of antiquity or, indeed, the move from horde to matriarchy to patriarchy, which Freud accepts in his reading of human history but for which he cannot account (Freud, 1913a: 149).

The absence of reflection on the mother is problematic. Freud tends not to engage with his postulation of the 'phallic mother' of the pre-Oedipal stage who provides the all-powerful context against which the child's individuality has to develop and with which it struggles. The Oedipus story could look quite different if more consideration were given to the power of the mother. As Bettelheim reminds us, in Sophocles's tale, Jocasta exposes Oedipus. This act reveals her power over life and death: a situation analogous to the mother's power to give or withhold food to the child. The simple, gendered dichotomy between fear (of the male) and desire (for the female) that dominates Freud's telling of this story fails to recognize the considerable ambivalence surrounding the figures of the mother and the father. The hated father is the one who, after his death, is desired; the mother/woman who is desired is also perceived as a threat. When Freud transfers the Oedipus story into the discussion of society, these ambiguities are further ignored. This has unfortunate consequences for the discussion of female sexuality. The mother who is associated only with sex and desire all-too-easily becomes idealized as the benevolent angel of so much Victorian fiction. Such idealizations leave the way open to fatal misunderstanding of real mothers (whose power to harm their children may be overlooked) or to the denigration of women who are seen to have 'failed' in their attempts to live up to the maternal ideal of the all-loving and self-sacrificing mother.

Moving the Oedipus complex into the realm of social history exacerbates some of the problems that we have already encountered in its application as a model for understanding psychosexual identity. Transferred to the historical realm, its masculine bias is exposed. Lacan famously suggested there was no such thing as 'Woman', for she merely reflects male attitudes and fears. Not surprisingly, perhaps, he also argues for the primacy of *Totem and Taboo* in the Freudian canon. Moving the complex into prehistory suggests some of the limits of Freud's model when it is taken to be a scientifically provable hypothesis. A better solution might be to pursue Ricoeur's identification of the primal murder as a 'myth', a creative way of presenting some of the psychic tensions, fears, and desires that Freud locates in every individual's relationship with his or her parents.

We need stories to engage with the fabric of our lives; what Freud does most effectively is provide stories which aid reflection on the forces that have formed us. What happens when one story is given too much weight? Is this what happens in Freud's account?

The move from the individual to society is completed by a final audacious use of the Oedipus story. Freud claims that there are two forces at work in the universe; forces that are played out on the bodies of individuals and in the experiences of collective society. These cosmic forces are *Eros* and *Thanatos*, Sex and Death. If Oedipus is the myth that exemplifies these features in the life of every individual, Freud's later writings take these features and make them central for understanding the conflicted nature of the human animal trapped in a universe defined by overwhelming, impersonal forces.

Eros and Thanatos: Oedipus and metapsychology

Freud's Oedipus complex moves from being a description of individual development to becoming a description of human society. In the final stage of his theorizing the themes of the story are taken still further as Freud develops an account of the cosmic forces which, he claims, are played out on the bodies of individual men and women.

In developing this idea, Freud draws upon the 'cosmic phantasy' (Freud, 1937a: 246) of Empedocles of Acragas (around 490–430 BCE), who he describes as 'an investigator and thinker, a prophet and a magician, a politician, a philanthropist and a physician' (Freud, 1937a: 245). Empedocles is, in other words, a polymath much like himself. According to Empedocles, two principles govern the life of the mind and the life of the universe: Love and Strife. Love is the uniting principle, while Strife seeks to 'separate the primal particles of the elements from one another' (Freud, 1937a: 246). Love involves growth and flourishing; Strife, entropy and destruction. The dynamic that shapes the story of Oedipus – love of the mother/hatred of the father; sex with the mother/ death of the father – is now used to shape an account of the nature of the universe. There is, however, a difference. Empedocles's account is mythical, while Freud's is based in 'biological validity' (Freud, 1937a: 245) and is thus scientific.

This is a highly controversial theory. In his more general theory, Freud sees human life as shaped by powerful instincts, most notably, the sex-instinct, which pushes for growth, new life, and development. Later, this postulation of one instinct that holds all in thrall is accompanied by the idea of a 'death-instinct' that seeks to break things down and to lead the animate back to an inanimate state. Freud's emphasis on the instincts for understanding individual character and behaviour has been largely superseded in the psychoanalytic theories that come after his death, which focus on 'object-relations'. In such theories, the child's relationship with its parents, not instinctual forces, is central for understanding how we shape our lives and our subsequent relationships. In Freud's later ideas, a not-dissimilar shift can be discerned, although it is left to others to complete this move. What we can say is that as his theory develops, more weight is placed on the role the external world plays in shaping individual identity (Freud, 1923a).

Accompanying this shift from the instincts to a focus on the external world is a desire to understand the apparently illogical and irrational sources of human destructiveness. Rather than relate this solely to failures in the processes of individual development, Freud seeks a broader explanation. In this sense he never moves beyond his claims that human nature unfolds against the backdrop of the instinctual pressures that drive our behaviour. At the outset of his theory, the instinct that drives human behaviour is that which seeks pleasure: the pleasure-principle, linked to the sex-instinct (Freud, 1911). But as he seeks to understand destructiveness, focusing on this one instinct does not seem to make sense. There seems to be another principle at play, which seeks destruction, not pleasure. This he describes as 'the death-instinct'.

Critics have resisted this idea. Psychoanalysts have similarly distanced themselves from accepting the existence of this instinct. The analyst Donald Winnicott suggested that it showed Freud's indebtedness to the Judeo-Christian tradition, the death-instinct acting as 'a simple reaffirmation of original sin'. Like sin for Christians, death becomes a negative force passed down through the generations. Yet to reject it in this way is, perhaps, to miss the strength of some of the evidence that Freud presents for it.

In the previous chapter we saw Freud engaging with the theoretical implications of the broken analysis with Dora. In 'the negative therapeutic reaction' the patient, apparently without explanation, seeks to sabotage the success of an analysis. Just at the point where real progress is possible, they return to the destructive patterns and behaviours that led them to analysis in the first place. Why? No pleasure would seem to attend to such a return. What might be behind such repetitions?

In children's play, Freud sees repetition as an attempt to master anxiety. In a game played by his grandson, Freud notes that as he throws out a cotton reel he says '*fort*' ('go') and as he draws it back he says '*da*' ('there'). Freud concludes that this game enables the child to master his anxiety at his mother's absence (Freud, 1920: 14–16). His mother is the cotton reel and in play he imagines himself to be in control of her comings and goings. Freud offers this example in the context of his discussion of the pleasure-principle. The pleasure-principle seeks to maximize pleasure and avoid 'unpleasure'. As the child grows, the reality-principle emerges as it realizes its wishes cannot always be met. (The word 'no', sadly, enters into the child's experience.) In light of this realization, the child begins to accommodate the external world, its disappointments and limitations.

We could read Freud's grandson's game in this way. Repeating the absence of the mother even in play seems distressing and at odds with the idea that all actions aim at maximizing pleasure. Yet, as Freud points out, this game turns a passive experience into an active one. The child takes control. At the same time, a form of revenge against the absent mother can be entertained in the form the play takes. The child is 'able to repeat his unpleasant experience in play because the repetition carried along with it a yield of pleasure of another sort but none the less a direct one' (Freud, 1920: 16).

But – crucially – not all repetitive actions can be so easily explained. In the 'traumatic neurosis', the sufferer's dreams repeatedly locate him in the place of the original trauma (Freud, 1920: 13). There is no movement, no sense of mastery over the traumatic event. Such repetitions not only defy the idea that all actions attempt to maximize pleasure but also the notion that all dreams are wish-fulfilments. Considering this phenomenon leads

Freud to suggest an instinct 'beyond the pleasure-principle'.
More than that: it leads to a radical reformulation of what an
instinct is. '*An instinct*', he notes, '*is an urge inherent in organic life to
restore an earlier state of things*' (Freud, 1920: 36). This is an important shift and Freud notes that this new definition is likely to
sound strange:

> We have become used to see in [instincts] a factor impelling
> change and development, whereas we are now asked to recognise
> in them the precise contrary – an expression of the *conservative*
> nature of living substance (Freud, 1920: 36).

Freud suggests there is an instinct that predates sex itself. This
drive to restore things to an earlier state is witnessed in the processes of death, where the animate returns to an inanimate state.
Freud argues that this primeval instinct resides at the very heart
of the organism:

> If we take it as a truth that knows no exception that everything
> living dies for *internal* reasons – becomes inorganic once again –
> then we shall be compelled to say that 'the aim of all life is death'
> (Freud, 1920: 38).

This staggering claim goes some way to explaining the compulsion to repeat, the experience in which this instinct is most
keenly felt. The subject is unable to move beyond the past experience that is constantly reformulated and repeated. There is a
sense of stagnation; a feeling that life itself is being obliterated.
If you think this sounds far-fetched, think about the all-too-
common example of people who seem to repeat, obliviously, the
same pattern of relationships, constantly entering into relationships or situations that can only turn out badly.

What causes this self-destructive behaviour? Freud's reflections
on a form of the compulsion to repeat which he calls the 'fate

neurosis' are particularly interesting for clarifying what he is getting at:

> The impression [such patients] give is of being pursued by a malignant fate or possessed by some 'daemonic' power; but psychoanalysis has always taken the view that their fate is for the most part arranged by themselves and determined by early infantile influences (Freud, 1920: 21).

As with traumatic dreams, there seems to be no obvious yield of pleasure from pursuing the same destructive behaviours. Yet appealing to a malignant force outside the patient is in tension with the primacy given by psychoanalysis to the unconscious and its power to influence behaviour. It cannot be that an external fate is driving the patient on; it is just that the factors that have determined such behaviour have been repressed and excluded from memory.

A similar idea informs Freud's reflections on Sophocles's attempt to soften Oedipus's 'hideous' crime so that his audience might engage with it. Oedipus is portrayed as a victim of fate, at the mercy of forces beyond his control. In portraying Oedipus in this way, Sophocles is 'projecting the hero's unconscious motive into reality in the form of a compulsion by a destiny which is alien to him' (Freud, 1928: 188). Yet Oedipus never claims that anyone other than himself is responsible for his actions. On the contrary, 'his crime is acknowledged and punished as though it were a full and conscious one' (Freud, 1928: 188). This might seem unjust but Freud notes that 'psychologically [it] is perfectly correct' (Freud, 1928: 188). Oedipus is guilty, as at one time he did desire to sleep with his mother and kill his father! In both examples, despite appearances to the contrary, the individual determines their fate: it is just that they do not remember the events that have initiated such action.

This sounds rather different from what Freud appears to suggest when he connects the compulsion to repeat with the death-drive. In making this connection, Freud claims that there is something beyond the individual's experience – a force older than humanity itself – that is influencing the individual's actions; this is termed 'the death-drive'.

Not surprisingly, given this complex history, the death-drive remains a controversial piece of theorizing. Even Freud was not entirely convinced that his speculations were correct (Freud, 1920: 59). But this theme suggests, at the very least, something of the concerns that shape Freud's theory. He is not only considering the forces of individual development but is also seeking what we might call, with him, 'a metapsychology' that locates the human psyche in the broader ebb and flow of the cosmos. By thinking in these terms we might consider Neville Symington's claim that Freud is influenced by the ideas of the philosopher and psychologist Franz Brentano (1838–1917), whose lectures Freud attended as a young student. For Brentano, the mind is in touch with the external world and develops its ideas through direct contact with it. Symington suggests that Freud is influenced by this idea, despite failing to refer to Brentano.

Symington may have a point. Like Brentano, Freud is attempting to locate the individual and their mental processes in the larger ebb and flow of the universe. To do this – to think cosmically – he needs stories that will provide dramatic frameworks for his speculations; stories that transcend mundane human experience. Here, Freud the sceptical scientist meets the Freud who seems to have more in common with a religious visionary. Life is never just about growth and flourishing; it also involves decay and death. The timeless conflict to which Empedocles draws our attention and that forms a framework for Freud's speculations is played out in the human realm and in the individual. In the clinical setting, the question becomes one of how to move beyond the repetition of the death-drive in our lives and our experience. But more than that, it raises questions of how to live in a universe like this; a universe that involves the pain of death as well as the pleasure of sex. Far from being an irrelevance, Freud's speculations challenge us to think about the meaning of our lives, played out against the backdrop of a complex universe that can both be experienced as something beautiful and also as something which has the power to terrify.

4

Dreams, development, and the psyche

Our explorations of hysteria and the Oedipus complex have mapped the shifting currents that shape Freud's thought. His ideas are not set in stone but are open to change: not surprising, given that these theories are being developed over a lifetime. Similarly, the account of the mind that he develops is also open to revision, though one aspect remains constant: the importance he ascribes to unconscious processes in forming and shaping the self. Experiences and feelings that are difficult to deal with can be driven from consciousness but that does not mean that they cease to influence behaviour. In the case of the hysteric, they contribute to the development of their illness. In the case of psychosexual development more generally, the powerful phantasies of childhood concerning the nature of sex and our relationship with our parents continue to shape sexuality into adulthood.

Freud's interest may lie with exploring the unconscious but that does not mean that his account of it and its relationship to other mental agencies is somehow static; like the development of his ideas on hysteria and sexuality, his views shift and change over time. According to the commentators Richard Wollheim and Joseph Sandler, in the course of his career Freud moves between three models of the mind. The first, in the period around the mid-1880s, shapes his thoughts and underpins his account of hysteria. As Sandler puts it, under this model, 'the pent up unconscious forces leading to the symptom were thought of as affects or emotions that had been aroused by real traumatic events'. The repressed emotions associated with a traumatic moment are expressed as symptoms. As we have seen, Freud becomes dissatisfied with this 'affect-trauma' model and replaces it with a 'topographical' model; aptly named, as his theory now focuses on mapping what we might think of as the terrain of the mind. Under this approach, the mind consists of three systems, the conscious, preconscious, and unconscious. This model enables Freud to explore ideas of psychic energy moving between different systems. Significantly, it is a model that helps shape his work on dreams. It stays largely intact until 1923, when his language shifts again and he focuses on how to describe the 'structures' of the mind: the ego (the rational self), the id (the repository of unconscious desires), and the superego (the internalized voice of parental and cultural attitudes). When we think of Freud's theory, this structural model is most likely to be the one that comes to mind.

Why does this shifting terminology matter? It matters because recognizing these stages in his theorizing reflects different ways in which Freud can be read. For some, that which is last is obviously the most important for how we read him and understand the direction of his theory. When James Strachey translated Freud's work into English, he took Freud's last formulations and used them to shape the presentation of his earliest writings, thus giving a more coherent structure to the development of his ideas. The Standard English translation thus gives little indication that Freud is groping to create a new language through which to express his revolutionary claims about the human person. Neither does it suggest a process involving trial and error.

For some, the desire for coherence and consistency should be resisted and this has led to a different account of how to read Freud. The recent Penguin project to produce a new set of translations of Freud's work – under the general editorship of the

British psychotherapist and writer on psychoanalysis Adam
Phillips – is partly inspired by the desire to illuminate the gaps
and tensions in Freud's work that result from creating a new
language. Under a reading of this kind, it is not necessarily the
case that the last stage of Freud's theorizing should be seen as
definitive. It may well be that some of his earlier ideas are particularly useful for interpreting certain phenomena, and returning to earlier models might well be useful for the day-to-day
work of analytic therapy.

Emphasizing the progressive development in Freud's theorizing (from one (inadequate) theory towards another (more adequate) theory) fits well with the dominant way of reading him in
the British psychoanalytic tradition. Under this reading, he is a
developmental psychologist who frames psychosexual development as a movement from one stage to another. We might think
of the movement from oral to anal to genital stage in his model
of sexual development. Or we might think of the movement to
make that which is unconscious, conscious. The possibility is held
out for progression from the chaos of the unconscious world to
the order of the rational world of consciousness.

French psychoanalysis has been less convinced of the power
of this developmental, progressive model for understanding the
revolutionary nature of Freud's theory of human being. French
analysts, following the work of Freud's self-styled successor,
Jacques Lacan, emphasize Freud's early rather than his later writings. For example, Lacan argues that the most important aspects
of Freud's theorizing were his dream interpretation (1900); his
discussion of parapraxis, slips of the tongue (1901) and jokes
(1905c); and his attempt to detail the peculiar world inhabited by
the hysteric (1893–5, 1905a). For Lacan, it is this Freud, concerned to describe the strangeness of human experience, the
Freud who maps the uncertain terrain of the unconscious, who
is most important. Lacan is less interested in the later Freud who
sought to understand the workings of the ego and who saw the

work of therapy as a means of bolstering the fragile rational self against the onslaught of the unconscious (Freud, 1923a).

Following Lacan's reading, a particular tension in the human experience of time and history, highlighted by Freud, comes to the fore. Our mental life is such that the concerns of the past, the present, and the unknown future press in on us, informing and constructing our experience at every turn, often in conflicting ways. If we take this backdrop seriously, it is difficult to talk with confidence about psychic progression. As the French psychoanalyst André Green argues, the past is never straightforwardly put aside and memory is never a simple remembrance of past events. Similarly, the contemporary psychoanalyst and academic Rosine Perelberg points out that 'repetition, irreversibility and oscillation are all present in the functioning of the mind'.

Recognizing the existence of the unconscious necessitates accepting a more complex view of the experience of time. The conscious self is aware of the passing of time, the effects of the ageing process, the existence of the individual in a particular historical moment. It is not the same in the world of the unconscious. As Freud writes, 'There is nothing in the id that corresponds to the idea of time; there is no recognition of the passage of time and … no alteration in its mental processes is produced by the passage of time' (Freud, [1932] 1933: 74). In this sense, we are creatures who are both shaped and not shaped by the passing of time.

For Green, recognizing these two contrary perspectives has profound implications for how Freud's ideas are understood. He sees Freud as presenting a view of human life that cannot be fully understood by reference to the sequential, lineal progression of external time. And that has to be so, given that he emphasizes the existence of the unconscious. The timeless unconscious is not constrained by the movement from past to present but slips effortlessly between both, while anticipating our hopes for the future. The notion of developmental progress may well be an important factor for understanding the nature of human being but to accept Freud's postulation of the unconscious means that progressive development cannot be seen as the only factor in shaping our experience as human beings. In the psychic world, what is past is never totally put aside, for it co-exists with present concerns and with hopes for the future.

This overlapping sense of time becomes most evident when interpreting dream material. Dream-analysis plays an important part in the development of psychoanalysis, alongside the investigation of hysteria, for it is through dreams that Freud provides another way of enabling entrance into the mysterious world of the unconscious. At the same time, dreams reveal present and past concerns that are interlaid and overlapping, that distort and inform each other, suggesting that the psychoanalytic theory of time cannot be avoided if the unconscious is to be mapped and understood.

Dreams and the construction of the self

In considering dreams and the role they play in understanding the complex account of the self that Freud develops, we might profitably build upon the analysis made of Dora's dreams in Chapter 2. Then, dreams were seen as vital both to understanding the shape of Dora's illness and also as a means of revealing her intentions. By shifting our attention to one of Freud's own dreams, we are able to get a sense of why some psychoanalysts are not entirely happy with the idea that Freud's last account of the mind is the most authoritative. The topographical model, against which his theory of dreams develops, might well be seen as enabling greater attention to be paid to the movement in dreams than the rather more rigid structural model of the final stage of his thought. At the same time, analysing one of Freud's dreams illuminates the timelessness of the unconscious and the effect this might have on how we understand ourselves.

On the night of 23–4 July 1895 Freud had a dream that proved to be one of the most important in the history of psycho-analysis. We get some sense of its significance from a letter to his friend Wilhelm Fliess, written five years later. Visiting the house where he had this dream, Freud wonders whether 'some day a marble tablet will be placed on the house inscribed with these words – "In this House, on July 24th, 1895 the Secret of Dreams was revealed to Dr. Sigm. Freud"' (Freud, 1900: 121n).

This dream, known in psychoanalytic history as the 'dream of Irma's injection', is the first dream that he submits to a full psychoanalytic interpretation. Through this detailed analysis he provides a model for future dream interpretation, as well as iden-tifying the processes of the unconscious. Freud's analysis con-tends that dreams are multi-layered phenomena that need to be worked with to be read. Material that connects current concerns with events long buried in the psyche can be discerned if the content of dreams is rigorously explored. In the case of the dream of Irma, the power of the unconscious to know more about one's current dispositions than perhaps one is prepared to accept at the time of the dream itself is also revealed. The ghostly presence of Freud's friend Wilhelm Fliess haunts this dream and suggests something of Freud's conflicted feelings towards this friend. These feelings are not accepted in his interpretation but if we consider the afterlife of the dream they are illuminated when it is remembered years later and the friendship is over.

The model that Freud provides for interpreting dreams begins with a description of the context for the dream. It comes during his analysis of a young woman in the summer of 1895. Freud notes some of the personal tensions surrounding this case. The patient is 'on very friendly terms with me and with the family' and, he goes on to note, 'It will be readily understood that a mixed relationship such as this may be a source of many dis-turbed feelings in a physician and particularly in a psychothera-pist' (Freud, 1900: 106). Of particular concern is the effect that any failure in the analysis might have on his relationship with the patient and her family. And this is a real concern; to date, the analysis has not been going particularly well. Freud notes its 'partial success' (Freud, 1900: 104), but while his patient has been relieved of some of her hysterical anxiety, some of her symptoms remain. The treatment has been broken off for the summer break. At this point Freud has a visit from Oskar Rie, a junior colleague who has recently seen this patient. Rie comments – none too favourably – on the health of the patient, now identified as 'Irma'. Freud feels he is being criticized, although at the time he is not aware of the depth of his feelings about this apparent reproof. He is, however, sufficiently perturbed to write out a history of her case with the intention of giving it to another friend and colleague, Josef Breuer, 'in order to justify myself' (Freud, 1900: 104). These concerns and fears are the real-life events that shape the content of the dream.

The dream begins with Freud receiving guests, one of whom is Irma, in a large hall. He reproaches her for not accepting his solution to her illness and tells her, 'If you still get pains, it's really only your fault.' She responds by saying that she is suffering from terrible pains in her throat, stomach, and abdomen. Freud is alarmed by her appearance – she is pale and puffy – and takes her to a window to get a better look at her. She resists his attempts to look down her throat and he attributes this to the kind of 'recalcitrance' shown by women who wear dentures. This unwillingness to co-operate irritates him. Eventually, she opens her mouth properly and he finds a white patch with 'whitish grey scabs upon some remarkable curly structures which were evidently modelled on the turbinal bones of the nose'. Freud calls in 'Dr M' (the alias he gives his friend and colleague Breuer) who repeats the examination and confirms it. Freud notes that Dr M does not look the same as he usually does – he is pale, walks with a limp, and is clean-shaven. His friends 'Otto' (Oskar Rie) and 'Leopold' (Ludwig Rosenstein) now join him. Leopold examines

Irma 'through her bodice', noting that 'she has a dull area low down on the left'. He also notes that the skin on the left shoulder is similarly infected. Dr M comments that, 'There's no doubt it's an infection but no matter; dysentery will supervene and the toxin will be eliminated.' The source of this infection is clear: Otto had not long before given her an injection of 'propyl, propyls … propionic acid … trimethylamin'. Freud thinks that such a thing should not be done thoughtlessly, concluding that 'probably the syringe had not been clean' (Freud, 1900: 107).

This, then, is what Freud calls the *manifest content* of the dream. What he has given is a straightforward description. He notes the connection to the events of the previous day. While there is clearly some connection, those events do not enable every aspect of the dream to be understood. Why the astonishing set of symptoms that Irma presents? Why the 'senseless' injection? Neither dream event can be traced to the events of the previous day. Freud finds the dream perplexing and thinks that 'towards its end the dream seemed to me to be more obscure and compressed than it was at the beginning' (Freud, 1900: 108).

Interpreting the dream is far from straightforward. Its meaning is obscure, not transparent. To discern its meaning, a detailed analysis of the dream is required. Freud seeks to discover the dream's *latent content*; in other words, he looks for the meaning that lies beneath its component parts. At this point we might wonder why we need to assume any meaning other than that which the dream presents. Given the obvious connections to the events of the previous day, couldn't it simply be understood as the mind playing with those events? Freud refutes this suggestion, claiming that if the work of analysis is undertaken, surprising things come to light that cannot be explained in this limited way.

So Freud begins. He breaks the dream down into its component parts so that each part of the dream can be scrutinized. He adopts this approach because he believes dreams to be *composite formations* (Freud, 1900: 104): the material that comprises the dream can be shown, when analysed, to be drawn from a range of sources and periods in the subject's life. This varied content is employed to mask the central idea or feeling that is emerging from the unconscious. At the time he is writing *The Interpretation of Dreams*, Freud is working with the topographical model of the mind. This model suggests a psychic movement where what is unconscious presses towards consciousness. For an unconscious thought to become conscious, it has to first become 'preconscious'; able, in theory, to be examined and understood. This 'preconscious' material becomes available – albeit in disguised form – in dreams. It is disguised to evade the process of censorship by which such disturbing material has been repressed in the first place and thus rendered unconscious. But through taking on this obscure form it has sought to escape the processes of repression and is now open to the possibility of being made conscious if interpreted.

To access this hidden material, Freud employs the method of free association that he developed through his work with hysterics. The content of each segment of the dream is subject to this relaxed reflection. Whatever enters the mind is considered, regardless of its character or its perceived relevance to interpreting the material of the dream. A painstaking analysis of all the dream's individual elements follows, although, as we shall see, there is a sense in which crucial elements of this analysis are not presented in the text and are only revealed later in Freud's private correspondence.

The construction of Irma in the dream is particularly important for revealing the timelessness of the unconscious. Freud quickly realizes that the 'dream Irma' is not simply to be identified as his troublesome patient. This realization begins as he notes the difference in complexion between the 'real' Irma, who has rosy cheeks, and the 'dream' Irma, who is pale-faced. Reflecting on this difference, Freud begins to suspect that 'someone else was being substituted for her' (Freud, 1900: 109). Far from 'Irma' representing just one other woman, further connections suggest a number of women lie beneath this dream woman. These include Freud's wife 'Martha' and a friend of Irma's, whom Freud suspected was also a hysteric but who he felt would be more amenable as a patient than the real Irma. In the terms of the dream, this newcomer would open her mouth properly in order to 'swallow' his diagnosis (Freud, 1900: 111). The composite Irma reveals an important aspect of Freud's claims about dreams: they are *over-determined*. Many layers are superimposed, to mask the unconscious desire or thought that is being driven towards consciousness. Once subjected to interpretation, these attempts to disguise an unacceptable feeling or thought reveal significant concerns.

When Freud presents his analysis in *The Interpretation of Dreams*, surprisingly he shies away from exploring those aspects of the dream which suggest sexual elements at work. Noting that Irma is examined 'in spite of her dress,' he deliberately ignores the erotic charge of examining a female patient through her clothes, although this comment does remind him of a doctor who seems to have got into trouble on precisely this point. But when thinking about what this connection might mean about his desires, his response is surprisingly puritanical: 'I had no desire to penetrate more deeply at this point' (Freud, 1900: 113). A strange lack of interest in sexual matters, and a response that sits uneasily with the importance he ascribes to sexuality. But this is early in his career, at a time when he is striving to make these new ideas acceptable to a broader – though not necessarily more broad-minded – audience. In a letter to his fellow psychoanalyst Karl Abraham, written some time later, in 1908, Freud returns to the sexual aspect of this dream. He is prepared to share with Abraham his reflections on the number of women who make up the composite (*Sammelperson*) Irma: 'sexual megalomania is hidden behind it ... I have them all!' 'Swallowing' a diagnosis and a physical examination, in the private realm of the letter, take on a more sexually charged tone, suggesting that there are further layers of meaning waiting to be explored in the content of one dream.

This omission suggests a further problem with the method by which Freud establishes the existence of the unconscious. It stems, as we have seen, from his attempts to understand the symptoms of the hysteric and also from his self-analysis of which his dream investigations form a part. But in the psychoanalytic theory and practice that he goes on to develop, the kind of analysis to which he is submitting the Irma dream would require the presence of an analyst. This is important, for this second person can question and query the dreamer's interpretations, pressing them on just the kind of disturbing associations that Freud wishes to avoid.

In *The Interpretation of Dreams*, the analysis takes a further disturbing turn. Freud considers the second examination by Dr M, who he decides has the appearance of his elder brother, with whom he had recently disagreed. This sense of being at odds with someone is mirrored in a troubling experience he had as a young doctor. Freud had prescribed a substance – sulphonal – then considered harmless, to a woman who was, as a result, severely poisoned. A senior colleague had to be called in to deal with the aftermath. Freud notes that the patient's name was Mathilde, a name shared with his eldest daughter, who had recently recovered from a serious illness:

> It had never occurred to me before but it struck me now almost like an act of retribution on the part of destiny. It was as though the replacement of one person by another was to be continued in another sense: this Mathilde for that Mathilde, an eye for an eye and a tooth for a tooth (Freud, 1900: 112).

Not for the last time, Freud makes a near-religious connection between two different people or events (a theme to which we will return in the next chapter). But note that Freud claims he had not considered this connection between the two Mathildes before having the dream. Something new is being played out through the dream's content.

This stage in the analysis opens up what seems to be its main concern. Remembering an experience of past incompetence raises a particular anxiety. Is he really a good doctor? To understand this anxiety takes us to the heart of *The Interpretation of Dreams*: Freud claims that all dreams are wish-fulfilments, hence their importance, physiologically and psychologically. They offer the pleasure of seeing our wishes fulfilled, to ensure the sound sleep required physiologically for good health. They are psychologically significant, because they offer access to the unconscious wishes of the individual. This leaves a question mark over nightmares and dreams that repeat traumatic experiences. Not straightforwardly wish-fulfilments, they lead Freud, as we have seen, to that which lies 'beyond the pleasure-principle': the death-drive found in repetition and the desire to return all things to an inanimate state.

The Irma dream, however, is a straightforward example of a wish fulfilled. Freud wishes to be seen as a good doctor. In a nutshell, the dream has this message: 'Yes, I am a good doctor; the problem is with the patient.' But in designating the dream as the fulfilment of a wish, Freud also reveals something of the unconscious, which knows more than our conscious selves about our attitudes, desires, fears, and anxieties. This is brought into sharp relief when the aspects of the dream that he neglects in his analysis are considered.

The issue of medical malpractice unfolds against the backdrop of Freud's difficult and intense friendship with Wilhelm Fliess. Fliess was the first of the intimate male friends with whom Freud shared the development of his ideas. An ear, nose, and throat specialist, Fliess forged a powerful bond with Freud that, later, Freud was to view as redolent of unacknowledged homosexual feelings. At the time of the dream of Irma's injection, Fliess was the person with whom Freud shared most about the psycho-analytic enterprise on which he was embarked. In the dream itself, Fliess is an anonymous presence, identified only through the mention made of the chemical formula of the injection, which includes trimethylamin. This substance Freud associates with Fliess, for Fliess argued that trimethylamin was connected with the chemistry of sexual processes (Freud, 1900: 116).

There is a further, more troubling connection between Fliess and the content of the dream, which Freud omits to reveal. One of Freud's patients was a woman called Emma Eckstein. In addition to other hysterical symptoms, she experienced frequent nosebleeds; Freud became concerned that this bleeding might have a physio-logical cause. He asked Fliess to examine her. Fliess did so and eventually operated on her nose. Far from improving Emma's con-dition, the bleeding intensified after the operation and was now accompanied by a terrible smell. A further examination by another doctor revealed Fliess to have left gauze in her nasal cavity. His negligence was thus responsible for exacerbating Emma's suffering.

If our source were only Freud's interpretation of the Irma dream, we would know next to nothing of this sequence of events. The structures in Irma's throat that look like nasal bones hint at Fliess's medical expertise and the underlying issue of professional standards intimates that – at least unconsciously – recognition of Fliess's carelessness is being played out. But in the dream, Fliess's thoughtless action is now Otto/Oskar Rie's mis-take, Freud going out of his way to deny any connection between his friend Fliess and medical misconduct.

Some years later, the relationship with Fliess broke down. At the time of the dream, the questions he seems to have had about his friend's character and behaviour are barely acceptable to his conscious self. Indeed, Peter Gay notes that in a letter written to Fliess a few hours after dreaming of Irma, Freud makes no men-tion of the dream that he clearly invested with such importance. Given Fliess's role as confidante, this seems surprising and suggests some awareness on Freud's part of that at which the dream hints. Revisited in the light of the later break in their friendship, the dream's message looks rather different from how it is presented in the published analysis. Read against later events, the dream could be seen as issuing a warning about a difficult and potentially dangerous friend. Read in this way, the dream suggests the unconscious is more aware of the conflicts with which we are struggling at a particular time than is the conscious self.

Considering the afterlife of this important dream suggests something about the creativity of the unconscious that cannot be reduced to the interplay between only past and present events. Some dreams have an almost prophetic quality that might suggest reasons for the common ancient idea that they foretell future events. Rosine Perelberg picks up this point, claiming that the first dream a client brings to analysis invariably reveals the shape of the future therapeutic relationship, as well as the issues that come to dominate it. Freud is far from comfortable with the idea that dreams presage the future: 'It would be truer to say instead that they give us knowledge of the past' (Freud, 1900: 621). Even if this were correct, it is important to recognize the way in which the past that has shaped us continues to inform present and future experiences. In the dream of Irma, the unconscious reveals itself to be ahead of Freud's conscious self in identifying the problematic nature of his relationship with Fliess and the failings of his friend. The problems of the relationship which disrupt its future are prefigured in the dream's unanalysed content.

Dreams suggest something of the fluidity of an account of the mind that takes seriously the idea of unconscious processes. The topographical model is particularly useful for this part of psychoanalytical work, as it enables the movement of psychic processes to be mapped, providing a useful screen against which interpretation can take place. But no interpretation can be fixed: given the notion of a timeless unconscious, there is considerable scope for interpretations to change over time.

In the dream of Irma, past, present, and future concerns and experiences are used to shape its narrative. This reveals something about human experience: it is never simply determined by present events, for past experiences both shape that present and the way in which our futures play themselves out. This complex interplay of different periods in our lives suggests something of the fragmentary nature of human selfhood. Our actions and feelings are never entirely transparent to our conscious selves. The unconscious, which also shapes us, is not limited by temporal continuity or coherence and can throw up ideas or feelings that our conscious selves struggle to identify. This means, as the French analyst Julia Kristeva powerfully puts it, that we are 'strangers to ourselves'. If we are to 'know ourselves', we need to recognize our location not only in time but also in the timeless world of unconscious processes. Nothing is completely put aside; nothing is ever really past. It is against this backdrop that the difficult work of character formation that shapes Freud's later reflections on ego and id takes place and there is nothing certain about its outcome. Establishing the self, under this model, is a precarious business but, as we shall see, it also offers creative possibilities for the human animal.

Time and the Wolf Man

Recognizing the complex construction of dreams suggests there is nothing straightforward about the workings of the unconscious. Dreams are over-determined; they use composite models that need to be carefully unpacked to get any sense of what the unconscious is seeking to reveal. Against this backdrop, becoming self-aware necessitates acquiring the kind of skills needed for reading a detective novel. Patience is required to follow the different twists and turns taken by the unconscious as it constructs its narrative. Significantly, these skills are needed not just for the interpretation of dreams but also for engaging with our memories.

In an early paper, 'Screen Memories' (1899), Freud considers the ability of the unconscious to shape our memories of the past. What we remember from childhood is not necessarily a straightforward representation of what actually happened. That which we remember often seems small and insignificant. Freud suggests that this is not the case. What we have in such memories are the results of struggles between the force that seeks to remember an important experience and another psychic force, which seeks to prevent it being made known. To come to the surface, an image for the original event is produced that replaces the original image.

In 'Screen Memories', Freud pursues a memory of playing in a meadow with his male and female cousins. The meadow is covered in yellow flowers, which they are picking together. He and his male cousin fall on his female cousin, snatching away her flowers. She bursts into tears and in consolation is given a piece of bread by a peasant woman who lives nearby. This would appear to be all rather straightforward.

But Freud is not convinced that this memory records an actual day in the country. For a start, why, from the many events of his past, does he remember this one with such clarity? Was it the taste of the bread; the colour of the flowers? He decides that there is 'something not quite right about this scene' (Freud, 1899: 312). He realizes that he did not always remember this playful event. It seems only to have come to mind when he was seventeen and in love for the first time. The object of his affections has returned to school and he is moping. He thinks particularly of her yellow dress. Three years later, plans to marry him to the cousin from the original memory come to nought but there is nostalgia in thinking how comfortable his life could be if they had. The memory is thus shaped by current concerns – a yellow dress, tasty home-made bread that could be his – rather than past events. More than that, this memory is shaped by the desires and emotions associated with the 'remembered' experience. The original scene, with its 'deflowering', suggests the sexual desires of childhood. Something is activated in the present that shapes the engagement with the past. As such, 'it may indeed be questioned whether we have any memories at all from our childhood: memories *relating to* our childhood may be all that we possess' (Freud, 1899: 322). Memories, like dreams, are far from straightforward. It is not so much the past that is being remembered as the present shaping our recollections of that past, and those present desires are themselves being shaped by the desires of the past. What we have in memory, as in dreams, is a complex weaving of different experiences, times, events, and emotions.

Some years later Freud returned to the question of how memory works. Why does a past event that was not experienced as traumatic at the time come back to haunt the subject at a later date?

This question arises in the case study of Sergei Pankejeff, immortalized as 'the Wolf Man', an evocative alias acquired from the dream that forms, as we shall see, the focus of his case. The Wolf Man's story is fascinating, not least because we know a lot about the shape his psychic life took after his analysis with Freud. Analysed by Freud between 1910 and 1914, and again in 1919, in 1926 he had a further period of analysis with Ruth Mack Brunswick. The analysis with Brunswick arose from a different set of problems, exemplifying something of the difficulty of accepting that any period of analysis could lead to a final 'cure' for all psychic ills. The original analysis with Freud and the later analysis with Brunswick provide powerful examples of the shifting time of the unconscious. What is of concern at one point in life might look rather different some years later.

Who was the Wolf Man and what brought him to Freud in the first place? The son of a wealthy Russian landowner, had been left Pankejeff by a gonorrhoea incapacitated and wholly dependent on others infection. When Freud introduces this case, he tells us that his intention is not to give a complete account of the analysis but to consider the patient's infantile neurosis as a way of illuminating aspects of child development. Until the age of ten, Pankejeff had suffered from an 'anxiety hysteria' which manifested itself as an animal phobia: he was terrified of horses. Over time, this phobia transformed into an obsessional neurosis, directed at religious observance and ritual. Freud describes the process that led to this transformation; a process which suggests something of the peculiar way in which time works in the psychic world.

At first glance, Pankejeff's childhood was unremarkable. His parents seemed happy until his mother began to suffer from various abdominal complaints and his father from depression. Looked after by a nurse who was extremely fond of him (his 'Nanya'), he was a quiet, well-behaved child, of whom it was often said that he should have been a girl. However, after he and his elder sister were left with an English governess one summer, his behaviour changed radically. On his parents' return, he was found to be 'discontented, irritable and violent' (Freud, [1914] 1918: 15). The blame for this change was levelled at the English governess and her difficult relationship with Nanya. A different source emerged in the analysis. During this summer, his sister had seduced him. This awakening of sexuality at the age of three and a quarter coincided with his discovery of the delights of masturbation and his nurse's threat to castrate him if he continued this pleasurable activity. Having seen his sister and one of her female friends urinating, he realized that neither had a penis. Struggling to understand this new-found knowledge of the female anatomy, he concluded that Nanya's threat was real. Coupled with his seduction, he developed a passive sexual identification, with a passive sexual aim: he derived pleasure from being punished and would do his utmost to get his father to punish him, to gain the masochistic sexual pleasure that he craved.

Considering the Wolf Man's childhood, Freud notes two phases. From three and a quarter to four years old, he was badly behaved and exhibited indications of perverse sexual desires: he enjoyed beating animals. This was followed by a phase during which he became increasingly neurotic and increasingly religious. The transition between these phases was marked by a dream. It is this dream that gives him his pseudonym but it also has wider significance for Freud's theorizing about the experience of time for the development of the mind.

> I dreamt that it was night and that I was lying in my bed. (My bed stood with its foot towards the window; in front of the window there was a row of old walnut trees. I know it was winter when I had the dream, and night-time.) Suddenly the window opened of its own accord and I was terrified to see that some white wolves were sitting on the big walnut tree in front of the window. There were six or seven of them. The wolves were quite white and looked more like foxes or sheepdogs, for they had big tails like foxes and they had their ears pricked like dogs when they pay attention to something. In great terror, evidently of being eaten by the wolves, I screamed and woke up (Freud, [1914] 1918: 29).

Freud asks Pankejeff to free associate around the elements of the dream. The wolves remind him of an illustration of a wolf standing on its hind legs, seen in a book of fairy tales. His sister mercilessly terrified him by showing him this picture. The tree also reminds him of a fairy story. In this tale, a tailor's house is invaded by a wolf. The tailor pulls off the wolf's tail and it flees. Later, the tailor meets the tailless wolf once more, this time with a number of other wolves. He hides in a tree. The wolves climb on top of one another to reach him but he scares them off by reminding them of the way in which he took the wolf's tail. The 'whiteness' of the wolves Pankejeff associates with a flock of sheep that he used to visit with his father and that died in an epidemic.

Important associations surround the window that opens of its own accord. Pankejeff wonders if this 'opening' relates to him opening his eyes. The dream feels terribly real and this suggests that it bears witness to something. Something is being remembered in the dream. This would seem to make sense. How many of us remember dreams from childhood? Evidently this dream made a powerful impression; so powerful that Pankejeff paints it. (The painting is housed in the Freud Museum in London.) Something of great significance is being expressed in the dream.

At this point in the case study, Freud breaks off his narrative to address his reader. He recognizes that the next part of the interpretation requires a considerable leap of the imagination, for he contends that the dream bears witness to something seen. At one and a half years old, Pankejeff saw his parents having sex. Suffering from malaria, Pankejeff had been sleeping in his parents' room. He wakes to see his father entering his mother from behind. Thus, he is able to see his mother's genitals. Beyond that, he does not understand what he has seen. It is only at the time of the dream – much later, when he is around four years old – that he is able to understand something of the scene, because of the sexual experiences and sexual researches that he has accrued since witnessing his parents' intercourse.

What we make of this claim will doubtless depend on the extent to which Freud's method of free-association is followed and the interpretations accepted. The wolf standing on its rear legs is the image of the father; the tailless wolf is an image of castration; the dead white sheep stand for punishment; the stillness of the wolves is a reversal of the movements made by his copulating parents (this reversal acting to mask that to which the dream refers). If we accept these connections we may well accept Freud's conclusion. If we don't, we won't.

What happens in the wake of the dream is what Freud deems significant. At this point the concept of *nachträglichkeit* ('deferred action'), becomes a significant theoretical tool. The French translation of *après-coup* for this phenomenon captures more clearly what concerns Freud. A kind of 'after-effect' (the literal translation of *après-coup*) occurs; it is this after-effect that Freud wishes to trace.

The dream marks a change in Pankejeff's behaviour but it brings more than that. The dream takes place as Pankejeff is starting to understand more about sexuality. Thus, it has to be seen in the context of the kind of sexual theories formulated by children that Freud articulates elsewhere (Freud, 1908b). As children develop, they become curious about what brings new children into the world. Their investigations may well be instigated by the attempt to account for the birth of an irritating younger sibling who has displaced them as the primary object of their parents' concern and affection. Parents tell tales of storks to explain the newcomer's presence, tales that the child quickly realizes cannot be true. They suspect that such tales hide a more disturbing reality, of which the parent refuses to speak. Seeking to fill in the gaps, they use aspects of their own experience to explain reproduction. Thus phantasies, fears, and desires come to shape their understanding of their parents and their relationship. Much later in his thought, Freud suggests the lasting power of these theories: they continue to be held long after the child receives 'sexual enlightenment' (Freud, 1937a: 234). Such is the creative and constructive power of the child's imagination.

We may be prepared to accept these claims. After all, children are curious and will develop theories to explain phenomena that parents do not wish to explain. We might even accept the tension between knowing the facts about sexual intercourse, while still being affected by the theories that one developed before knowing these facts. But Freud goes further, postulating specific conclusions that may be more difficult to accept.

This concerns his identification of a central infantile theory, held by boys, that all people possess a penis. Realizing a girl does not have a penis leads to the conclusion not that it was never there but that it has been removed. The fear of castration is thereby established (Freud, 1908b: 216–17). The violence of this imagined act finds parallels in the phantasies the child constructs about their parents' relationship. If sexual intercourse has been witnessed, or imagined, or constructed from noises in the parents' bedroom, it is likely to be interpreted as something violent, what Freud calls 'the sadistic theory of coitus' (Freud, 1908b: 221). Evidence for this theory might be provided if the child discovers spots of menstrual blood on the parents' sheets or the mother's knickers. Sex is constructed as a form of violation (Freud, 1908b: 221–2).

Applied to the Wolf Man's case, these violent theories provide explanations for the shape his phobia and the later neurosis takes. In the light of the new information the Wolf Man has about sexuality (imperfect and structured through phantasies as those infantile experiences might be), he wishes to take the place of the mother seen so many years ago and copulate with the father. However, the prohibition against masturbation is now in place, accompanied by the fear of castration, and so the desire has to be repressed. The desire for the father becomes fear instead and this is manifested in the animal phobia. The father, standing behind his mother as they have sex, takes on the form of the wolf he so fears.

According to Perelberg, this case study is important for how Freud understands the relationship between reality and phantasy; the world of facts and the inner world of the unconscious. To understand what drives the phobia and the obsessional neurosis of the Wolf Man, it is not enough to engage only with what he has seen but also with how what has been seen is, much later, interpreted. In other words, a web of phantasies, theories, and questions about the external world form in the child's imagination and, much later, reinterpret that which was seen in the past. This raises a crucial point about the relationship between phantasy and reality. It is not so much that the experience produces the phantasies. What this case suggests is that as these phantasies are formed they come to shape the way in which the external world is interpreted. That includes not just the present but the past as well. As Perelberg says, 'Freud raises a question concerning the extent to which it is factual history that produces phantasies and how far, on the contrary, the production of the event itself is governed by pre-existing phantasies'. This involves a fundamental reorientation concerning time. It is not so much witnessing his parents' love-making that creates a problem for the Wolf Man. What makes the scene problematic is when it is recalled against the development of his childish theories regarding sexual experience. So the castrated mother is bent to the father's will; he phantasizes about taking the mother's place; he fears that having these desires will lead his father to castrate him; and so on.

For Freud, psychosexual development cannot simply be reduced to the changing centres of pleasure, located in different bodily functions, that the child experiences. His is not a straight-forward form of developmental psychology. The child's experiences are always mediated through the phantasies and theories that emerge in response to his or her changing experience of the world. This necessitates a complex understanding of the relationship between real events and the imaginative re-workings of those events. Freud puts it thus:

> Scenes from early infancy ... are not reproductions of real occurrences, to which it is possible to ascribe an influence over the course of the patient's later life and over the formation of his symptoms ... Rather [they are] products of the imagination, which find their instigation in mature life, which are intended to serve as some kind of symbolic representation of real wishes and interests and which owe their origin to a regressive

tendency, to a turning-away from the tasks of the present (Freud,
[1914] 1918: 49).

This challenges the common criticism of psychoanalysis as
'obsessed with the past'. The past is a significant feature for
understanding the development of neurotic illnesses and also of
character. But it is never as straightforward an identification as
that. What the Wolf Man's case suggests is a more convoluted location of the individual in the world and in time. The significance of
past events can be reactivated in the present because something in
that present has made a past event look rather different. Memory
has been transformed, invested now with anxiety about the
meaning and possibilities of present relationships.

Psychoanalytic therapy: playing with time

The transformation of memory in the Wolf Man's case presents
creative possibilities for the therapeutic process. And perhaps it is
this connection to the practical work of therapy that makes the
reflections on time and the unconscious so interesting. The
psyche is flexible, not rigid. The meaning of the past is never
completely set in stone; in therapy the hope is that the past might
be experienced differently, enabling the possibility of change and
psychic growth.

The flexibility (or 'plasticity') of the psyche means human life
is never simply orientated towards the future. This has implications for the way in which the success of analysis might be
assessed. The phenomenon of *nachträglichkeit* suggests that the
past is never entirely put aside; there is always the possibility that
some past experience might be reactivated in the present.
This makes the idea of a lasting cure for psychic disturbance and
mental illness somewhat difficult to accept and towards the end

of his life, Freud grappled with the question of whether such a thing were really possible (Freud, 1937a).

The notion of a 'cure' for mental ills depends largely on an account of progression in the mind. It suggests that it is possible to deal, once and for all, with that which troubles us. The Wolf Man's case suggests a different momentum. His dreams act to reactivate the past. The possibility of such a regression suggests something about the peculiar processes of the unconscious. When we are awake, our focus is on progression: where we are going, how we are to get there, what we are to do. When we are asleep, the external world is not a feature of our immediate psychic experience and so there is the possibility of return to an earlier stage of our lives, exemplified in the material that forms our dreams. As a result, the past is a live presence, whose concerns can be brought to bear on the experience of the present.

As Freud discusses the notion of cure, the figure of the Wolf Man reappears. Freud mentions, perhaps with a degree of embarrassment, that this analysis was far from final. The new analysis with Brunswick has been necessary to deal with what Freud describes as 'residual portions of the transference' (Freud, 1937a: 218). In other words, it is not the past that continues to haunt Pankejeff, but aspects of the transference that he made to Freud. Brunswick – similarly uncomfortable with the idea that despite being treated by Freud his illness continues – reiterates Freud's claim that the focus of his time with her has been on 'an unresolved remnant of the transference' to Freud and resists the suggestion that what ails him can be conceived as the reappearance of something from childhood.

It is perhaps understandable that a nascent practice should wish to emphasize success in its therapeutic methods. But the reticence to consider that the basis of Pankejeff's illness might be traced to the re-emergence of something from childhood does some damage to the way Brunswick's analysis proceeds. Pankejeff arrives in her consulting room fixated on the idea that his nose is deformed. This physical complaint, not reflected in how his nose really looks, reflects powerful phantasies of persecution. When considering why this might be so, Brunswick connects his new malady with the same father-complex that structured the analysis with Freud. For Brunswick, the aim of the analysis is to enable Pankejeff to resist positioning himself as the passive female whereby he identifies with his mother's role in his remembrance of parental sex.

As the analysis progresses, Pankejeff is, indeed, more able to identify with his father. He can now achieve, according to Brunswick, a more active and appropriately 'masculine' position. What is neglected, however, is adequate discussion of the effect of his sister's seduction or his relationship with his mother. This is something of a missed opportunity, not least because Brunswick identifies a particular kind of transference in Pankejeff's relationship to her as a woman. And this connection seems significant, for through this unconscious identification, Pankejeff is able to address his tendency to take a passive or 'feminine' role in his relationships.

This makes the analysis with Brunswick rather different from that with Freud. The changed nature of the analytic setting offers the possibility of a new engagement with the past that has shaped one's identity: a man and a woman form a therapeutic partnership rather than two men. The different characteristics and character of the analyst, filtered through the patient's experience of the transference, enable new things to come to light. Pankejeff's fear of his father and his identification with his mother can now be considered without loss of self-esteem in the presence of the female analyst. In Pankejeff's case, this psychic change is reflected in a dream that he tells Brunswick:

> The patient stands looking out of his window at a meadow, beyond which is a wood. The sun shines through the trees, dappling the grass; the stones in the meadow are of a curious mauve shade.

The patient regards particularly the branches of a certain tree, admiring the way in which they are intertwined. He cannot understand why he has not yet painted this landscape.

The dream reflects aspects of his original dream of the wolves: the patient is looking out of a window on to a scene that includes a tree. But the landscape is different (there are curious mauve stones) and there are no wolves. Importantly, the twisted branches of the tree (suggesting the entwined limbs of a sexual embrace) are not viewed with horror but with pleasure: he decides he would like to paint this tree. Brunswick's interpretation is that Pankejeff is now at a point where he is able to countenance the possibility of a sexual relationship, not with fear but with plea-sure. The dream is hopeful, although Brunswick notes that the progress that it heralds is not so easily achieved in reality. Hardly surprising: the possibility of moving beyond the old afflictions is not as easy as we like to think. Addressing the tensions within the psyche does not necessarily or immediately lead to changes in behaviour.

If we return to Freud, he has much to say about the role luck plays in effecting a lasting psychic cure. In practice, it is impossi-ble to know how lasting such a cure will be, not just because current experiences may reactivate aspects of the past. What hap-pens to us also has a bearing upon our psychic health. In this way, we are dependent on the uncertain hand fate casts us. This raises the question of exactly what analysis can hope to achieve. As Freud's theory develops, it becomes less about 'curing' mental illness and more about how therapy can aid the development of character. What tools can analysis provide to enable the client to be better prepared for the trials and tribulations that life, inevita-bly, throws at them? Looked at in this way, psychoanalysis cannot only involve investigation of the unconscious (the focus of Lacanian analysis) but must also help strengthen the ego. Analysis has a dual role, helping the patient cope with disturbances thrown up by the unconscious, as well as with the experiences of life itself.

In the paper 'Remembering, Repeating and Working Through' (1914a), Freud provides a template for how to achieve at least a degree of lasting change. His focus is on the problem of destructive, repetitive behaviour. Confronted with such phenomena, analytic therapy can enable the cessation of such repetition through facilitating the work of remembering. In repetitive behaviour, 'the patient does not *remember* anything of what he has forgotten and repressed but *acts* it out' (Freud, 1914: 150). Most importantly, 'he reproduces it not as a memory but as an action; he *repeats* it, without, of course, knowing that he is repeating it' (Freud, 1914a: 150). The task of analysis is to make what is unconscious conscious, for what becomes conscious has less power to affect action. The transference of past impulses, phantasies, and relationships by the patient on to the analyst becomes the key to this process. For Freud, the compulsion to repeat is played out, not only in the external world but also in the analytic setting, with one crucial difference: in analysis, the past relationships replicated in the transference can be analysed and brought into consciousness. The past that so troubles the patient can be played with in the safety of the analyst's room, made known and remembered.

For later psychoanalysts like Melanie Klein, Betty Joseph, and Donald Winnicott, using the transference enables new situations to be created that open up the possibility of healing past hurts. Freud is less positive about such an outcome, as we saw in our discussion of Dora's case. At root, the transference is, for him, a form of resistance where past relationships are played out in the analytic setting, to thwart the possibility of change:

> The unconscious impulses do not want to be remembered in the way the treatment desires them to be, but endeavour to reproduce themselves in accordance with the timelessness of the unconscious and its capacity for hallucination (Freud, 1912: 108).

In this sense, 'the transference is itself only a piece of repetition' (Freud, 1912: 151). Yet even Freud acknowledges that it can be used to effect change through providing a 'playground' for analyst and patient:

> The main instrument, however, for curbing the patient's compulsion to repeat and for turning it into a motive for remembering lies in the handling of the transference. We render the compulsion harmless and indeed useful, by giving it the right to assert itself in a definite field. We admit it into the *transference as a playground in which it is allowed to expand in almost complete freedom* and in which it is expected to display to us everything in the way of pathogenic instincts that are hidden in the patient's mind (Freud, 1912: 154; my emphasis).

The ability to play with the forgotten past makes therapeutic success possible. The past that is being re-experienced in the transference is now open to consideration in a more reflective manner; it can be subjected to what Freud calls 'uncritical self-observation' (Freud, 1900: 103). Through playing out the experience in the analytic setting, it is now possible that, through re-experiencing the past in the transference, a more detached relationship can develop to that past. As Julia Kristeva notes, the analyst's role is to put the patient's disturbing phantasies into words so that they cease to be terrifying, thus enabling what she calls, 'the staging of the unconscious'. Freud says something similar:

> [The analyst] must get [the patient] to re-experience some portion of his forgotten life but must see to it, on the other hand, that the patient retains some degree of aloofness, which will enable him, in spite of everything, to recognise that what appears to be reality is in fact only a reflection of a forgotten past. If this can be successfully achieved, the patient's sense

of conviction is won, together with the therapeutic success that is dependent upon it (Freud, 1920: 19).

Therapy allows for a reflective attitude to develop, where the past is not some 'undiscovered country from whose bourn no traveller returns' (Hamlet, 3.1), not something unknown that should be feared but, rather, something that can be brought to consciousness and with which one can engage. It is far from certain, of course, that remembering will effect lasting cure, for patterns of relationship are difficult to break. Yet Freud holds out the hope that greater reflection on one's actions will enable a greater sense of control over one's life. The task of remembering is vital to his method and goes some way to countering the common view that focusing on transference as the repetition of the past is less creative than the later Kleinian view of the transference as the most significant aspect of psychoanalytic therapy.

For the new experience opened up by remembering to take hold, the past needs to be 'worked through'. In this way analysis can be paralleled with the process of mourning. Freud defines mourning as 'the reaction to the loss of a loved person, or to the loss of some abstraction which has taken the place of one, such as one's country, liberty, an ideal, and so on' (Freud, [1915] 1917: 243). The work of mourning is a response that seeks to move the mourner beyond the loss of the object, allowing them to put aside the energy (or libido) that has hitherto been attached to the lost object (Freud, [1915] 1917: 244). Mourning takes time. It is slow, gradual, not to be rushed. Eventually, reality-testing enables the mourner to establish a degree of detachment from what has been lost. But more than that:

> The ego, confronted as it were with the question of whether it shall share this fate [i.e. the death of the object], is persuaded by the sum of the narcissistic satisfactions it derives from being alive to sever its attachment to the object that has been abolished (Freud, [1915] 1917: 255).

The pull of life, the desire to live again, to be fulfilled in one's own life, enables the mourner to move on.

Freud identifies a similar process in analytic therapy. Past attachments and defences that inhibit one's life can be identified as no longer necessary or appropriate. New ways of living can be explored.

Freud's method and the unconscious

Reflection on the varied experiences of time and, most notably, the refusal of the unconscious to be constrained by that which is lineal reveals a Freud who is not only mapping the progress of human psychosexual development. His account is more complicated, as he allows the shifting movements of the psychic apparatus – movements which allow for regression as well as progress – to shape his account of human being. The topographical model that forms the basis for the middle period of his work might enable, as some suggest, this sense of movement to be captured more powerfully than the later model of psychic structures. The shifting nature of the mind means that the past is never simply past. Similarly, the present shapes and is able to shape our memory of our origins and experiences.

The complexity of our existence in time – past, present, and future – makes human life both difficult and creative. It is difficult, because we can become prey to past fears and desires, losing perspective, trapped by what is past. Yet our experience is also creative, for we can play with our past experiences and dreams, reshaping them in the light of the present and future.

Not surprising, then, that Arthur Miller, one of the greatest writers of the twentieth century, should suggest something of the creative potential of our overlapping and overlaid memories. Reflecting on memories from his childhood, he recognizes the ability of the mind to use them – and particularly the phantasies which surround these early experiences – to shape the imaginings of his adult life:

> The view from the floor, filled though it is with misunderstand-
> ings, is also the purest, the matrix whose content is so difficult
> to change later on. The impact of things seen and heard from the
> carpet is red-hot and returns with a far greater shock of truth
> when recalled because those visions are our very own, our pri-
> vate misunderstandings of reality shared by no one else and are
> thus the soil of poetry, which is our freedom to alter mere facts.

The creative potential of that engagement with the past shapes psychoanalytic practice. Playing with the past in the ana-lytic setting suggests the future might be reconfigured. That does not mean that the task of analysis is once and for all: the constant movement in the mind between past, present, and projected future makes this hope uncertain, at the very least. Strengthening the ego, however, enables us to address both the past and its effects and to face the future with some degree of confidence.

Engaging with the human experience of time – both the lineal time of life in this world and the timeless life of the unconscious – suggests a possible connection between Freud's psychoanalytic theories and religion. This might sound surprising: as we shall see in the next chapter, Freud is extremely critical of religious ways of thinking. Yet traditionally, religion has provided a variety of frameworks for addressing the concerns which arise from being creatures who are temporal yet who have the ability to transcend the experience of time through thought and reflection. While Freud was extremely critical of the religious impulse, he also recognized the human need to establish some way of making life feel meaningful. If his reflections on time and the unconscious invite us to think again about the forces that have created us, his criticisms of religion enables us to explore how we might place our lives in the broader structures of the cosmos.

5
Religion and fate

One of the best-known photographs of Freud shows him at his desk, surrounded by statues of gods and goddesses from his extensive collection of antiquities. This picture tells us much about why ancient stories, such as that of Oedipus, should play such a significant part in his theory, for they clearly reflect his interests. However, the photograph also suggests something of the tensions in Freud's discussion of religion. He may reject the gods and the religious claims that support them but those same gods and beliefs remain objects of fascination.

Just as there are differences of opinion about how Freud should be read in terms of his overarching theory, so there are differences of opinion about how he should be read on religion. For most commentators, he is religion's greatest critic; a thinker who revels in his status as an unbeliever and 'Godless Jew'. For a growing number of others, like James DiCenso, this is a rather simplistic picture of a more complex engagement.

DiCenso claims that a detailed reading of Freud's many texts reveals 'the Other Freud', who cannot quite put away his Jewish inheritance and is fascinated by all things religious. This fascination means he can never quite put aside the concerns that drive religious theorizing; most notably, the desire to come to terms with mortality as well as finding ways of coping with the change and unpredictability that defines life in this world. His inability to escape these concerns means he cannot entirely avoid engaging with the question of how to live. Hardly surprising: after all, his thought involves both theoretical and therapeutic interventions, both ideas and practice. In this way, his theory can be seen as touching the sphere often occupied by the religious and his critique contains within it the germs of his philosophy of life.

Freud's critique of religion

It is best to start an investigation of the contrasting claims about Freud's approach to religion by considering his criticisms of it. In Chapter 3, we saw how *Totem and Taboo* traced the development of religion to an historical act of patricide. Freud argued that the guilt felt by his sons for killing the father was transmitted through the ages into the subsequent structures of religion. Far from being a supernatural phenomenon that reflects the creation of the world by a divine being, religion is revealed as rooted in the actions and fears of human beings.

Totem and Taboo was written in 1913. Much later in his career, Freud revisited the question of religion in two works dealing with the psychological processes that accompany the creation of civilization: *The Future of an Illusion* (1927) and *Civilisation and its Discontents* (1930). Against this backdrop, Freud considers the role of religion and the forces that shape its development.

In applying his account of psychosexual development to the social realm, Freud focuses on the cost that living in society exacts on human beings. This might seem a strange idea. We are accustomed to think about the development of 'civilization' as a 'Good Thing'. We might think about the art, philosophy, and complex systems of government that have accompanied 'The Ascent of Man' – to use the title of Jacob Bronowski's famous television series – as our ancestors moved from primitive forms of society to the technological societies we now inhabit. While Freud is convinced of the progress brought about by science, he is rather more pessimistic about the experience of civilization for those who belong to it. According to his theory, civilization is not an unmitigated good and it is in this context that religion and its illusory comforts took shape.

How does he map the relationship between civilization and religion? Recognizing the natural world as not entirely support-ive of human beings, their hopes, and their dreams leads him to a particular view of human society. Humans are puny, defenceless creatures who can easily be destroyed by the power of Nature (Freud, 1927a: 15). One way of forming a defence against nature's onslaught is to live not in isolation, but in a community. In this social solution, Freud identifies a fundamental conflict for the human animal. If civilization is to survive, the instinctual desires for sex and violence have to be curbed. Civilized society will not survive if I pursue my desires with no concern for the effect this might have on others. Structures such as marriage and the family provide a framework that renders (reasonably) safe the power of these instincts. Rather than express these instincts freely, finding immediate gratification for them, their satisfaction is deferred. Sublimating such desires into other forms of action can bring some satisfaction, for example through the creation of art or the writing of philosophy (Freud, 1930: 97). That is not to ignore the tensions and frustrations that emanate from curbing such desires. If art and philosophy have come out of the attempt to limit the satisfaction of the instincts, religion similarly provides a form of compensation for that renunciation.

How does it do this? On the one hand, it takes natural forces and gives them a human face (Freud, 1927a: 16). Gods are created that reflect the power of nature. In this transformation, Nature ceases to be something cold and unfeeling and becomes something with which humans can communicate. If necessary, these gods can be appeased in the same way that another human being might be. The gods 'reconcile men to the cruelty of Fate' but they also 'compensate [men] for the sufferings and privations which a civilized life in common has imposed on them' (Freud, 1927a: 18).

The second point is particularly important for Freud. In the religious worldview, the painful and frustrating realities of existence are not the be-all and end-all of human experience. This world is not the only world open to human beings and religious systems of thought place meaning outside this world. In the religious universe, there is a 'spiritual world' beyond this one and the 'real' self is located in a soul that is separate from the fallible body and thus able to evade death. Nature is not 'blind' but cares for us; death is not the end of life but the gateway to a 'better' life (Freud, 1927a: 19). In this way, religious thinking enables human beings to psychologically protect themselves against 'the dangers of nature and Fate' (Freud, 1927a: 18). The world is no longer hostile; more than that, it is not the only realm in which we will live. Religion thus provides a form of compensation for the loss of the pleasures of this world by postulating a better world beyond.

Freud does not deny the psychological usefulness of these beliefs for life in a world that does not always seem kind. However, in the end these beliefs are fundamentally false. They may have made sense in a pre-scientific world but they must now be put aside. Religion is an anachronism in the modern world; failing to give up such ideas reveals a fundamental inability to accept the cold truth of reality.

This discussion of the forces that shape human society forms the context for the main thrust of Freud's critique. Religion is a form of illusion ill suited to the scientific age in which we live. What is an illusion? An illusion is something that reflects a human wish (Freud, 1927a: 31). It is not driven by evidence but by desire. Note that an illusion is not the same as a delusion. A delusion is a false belief. This need not be the case with an illusion, although Freud sometimes slips between the two meanings in his discussion of religion. While a delusion is always false, an illusion could (in theory) turn out to be true. Little Kate Middleton might have wished to marry a prince when she grew up; she might have believed it would happen. Years later, her wish comes true and she becomes Prince William's wife and Duchess of Cambridge. But – and this is the important point – it might equally not have happened. After all, most little girls who dream of marrying a prince are sadly disappointed! Freud's point is that illusory beliefs are not based in evidence but reflect wishes about the world. Just like the dream to marry a prince, religious beliefs are illusions because they are shaped by wishes about reality rather than evidence derived from it. We might note, as an aside, that Freud, too, uses the example of a girl dreaming of being a princess (Freud, 1927a: 31).

Illusions are powerful and long lasting because they reflect the earliest wishes of infancy. It is these wishes that Freud highlights in the illusions of religion. As the child grows, they experience anxiety, becoming aware of the reality of the external world that impinges on them. They look to the father to protect them, as he is the most powerful figure in their world. The same desire for protection is found in religious belief. Religion emerges from the psychological need for security; the believer finds in the figure of the father the basic material for the construction of a god:

> When the growing individual finds that he is destined to remain a child forever, that he can never do without protection against strange superior powers, he lends those powers the features belonging to the figure of his father; he creates for himself the gods whom he dreads, whom he seeks to propitiate and whom he nevertheless entrusts with his own protection (Freud, 1927a: 24).

Religion is thus a form of wish-fulfilment. It takes the wish for protection and, by postulating an all-powerful father-god, provides a fulfilment of that wish. In religious beliefs we are able to view the most basic desires of the human condition, for in them we have 'fulfilments of the oldest, strongest and most urgent wishes of mankind' (Freud, 1927a: 30).

This suggests that whatever else Freud's critique of religion does, it does not suggest that religious beliefs are meaningless. Far from it, for such beliefs reveal much about the fears and desires that drive human action. As Freud notes, 'religious beliefs give us information about what is most important and interesting to us in life' (Freud, 1927a: 25). Just as dreams – also, remember, understood as wish-fulfilments – enable access to the unconscious, so religion provides a rich resource for exploring the unconscious.

However, Freud is not nearly as positive about the exploration of religion as that connection suggests. Elsewhere, he identifies religion as a form of psychopathology. It is, if you like, a form of mental illness. Freud is specific in his diagnosis. Religion is a form of obsessional neurosis through which the individual seeks to control the world, in much the same way as the neurotic who constructs a series of repetitive actions or rituals to keep themselves safe. I might need to arrange my clothes 'just so' before I get into bed (Freud, 1907); in a similar vein, religious rituals act as ways of rendering safe an otherwise frightening world.

To an observer, the actions of the person suffering from an obsessional neurosis might appear meaningless but for the person themselves this is far from the case: 'any deviation from the ceremonial is visited with intolerable anxiety' (Freud, 1907: 118). The actions enacted by the neurotic are like mini-ceremonies; almost 'a "sacred act"' (Freud, 1907: 118). There is, in other words, a similarity between the actions of the obsessional neurotic and religious rituals, although Freud points out that these are not exactly the same, because the neurotic's actions do not have the public and communal quality of religious practice. They are, rather, forms of 'private religion' (Freud, 1907: 119).

Freud's exploration of such actions take place in his consulting room; his intention is to show how such actions relate to specific repressed events in the patient's life. These actions may be strange but when analysed they can be shown to provide ways of coping – however inappropriately – with unresolved issues and repressed instincts.

Let us return briefly to the Rat Man, whom we met in Chapter 3. Lanzer has developed a series of detailed plans and rituals that regulate his life. He comes to Freud because these rituals have become so all-consuming that he can no longer act at all in the world. Through the process of analysis, Freud shows these rituals relate to his desire to protect his loved ones from phantastical horrors that he imagines being inflicted on them. To an observer,

Lanzer's rituals might have seemed ludicrous but when analysed they are far from meaningless. During the course of the analysis they are traced back to the events and fears of his childhood and his difficult relationship with his father (Freud, 1909b). Freud's purpose in tracing these actions to their source in the past is to enable the patient's return to health. Once the origin of the obsessive act is revealed, the patient will be able to let go of the action.

A similar concern shapes his engagement with religion. Defining religion as 'a universal obsessional neurosis' (Freud, 1907: 127) leads Freud to conclude that its ritualistic actions and illusory beliefs can be traced to an original source. Identifying this source means that the power of religion will be broken. In part, Freud identifies human anxiety in the face of a threatening world as this source, although he provides historical basis for religious rituals in the guilt felt by the band of brothers for murdering their father (see Chapter 3). In telling this story, Freud undercuts the 'truth' of religion by revealing its source in a historical act that reverberates down the centuries. Once this source – or the source of religion in anxiety – is accepted, the claims of the religious can be rejected.

Freud's ideas on religion have been dismissed by thinkers from the worlds of philosophy, religion, and psychoanalysis. For philosophers of religion, like John Hick, Freud's account rests on exposing the roots of religion in psychological processes. Hick comments that this 'may be true but has not been shown to be so'. Describing the alleged origins of religion is one thing, assuming this leads to the conclusion that God does not exist is quite another. The psychological path Freud maps may be correct and his arguments may tell us much about how the concept of God held by any particular individual or society has developed over time. What his argument does not do, however, is conclusively show there to be no God.

For the philosopher and psychoanalyst Jonathan Lear, the main problem with Freud's argument is that he falls prey to his wishfulness for the end of religion. Freud thinks the western world has reached the stage when the illusions of religion can be put aside. Science can take over, creating a better world for everyone. Lear is damning: Freud is overly optimistic on this point and 'he suffers from an illusion of a future' without religion.

Others, such as Donald Winnicott, have sought a more positive rendition of the idea of illusion that lies at the heart of Freud's critique. Illusion is not something to be outgrown but part of the complex relationship that develops between self and world as we grow up. Our illusions shape our engagement with the world and others, just as our experience of the world and our relationships shape those same illusions. In this way, religion cannot easily be dismissed as something false that can be put aside as we achieve maturity. Winnicott sees religion as occupying the 'transitional space' that he places between self and world. Transitional space is connected to Winnicott's idea of the child's transitional object – a toy or object that the child identifies both with itself and the world beyond. In the transitional space that emerges from this – the space that is both 'me' and 'not-me' – Winnicott places creativity, imagination, and religion. This is the space for play. For Winnicott, religion provides rich sources for playing with the relationship between self and the world that surrounds the individual. If we accept this idea, there might be a rather different way of thinking about religion, even if, with Freud, we accept that it relates to human wishes about the world and our place in it. Religion becomes less a form of science, providing facts about the world, and more a form of creativity.

Religion, superstition, and the need to connect

The notion that religion is opposed to and inevitably fails in the face of science pervades Freud's critique. Not surprisingly, this characterization leads him to connect religion and superstition. While modern science is based on empirical evidence and reason, superstition and religion are not. In religion and superstition, the wish is more important than the evidence. The wish that is common to both is the wish for safety. Superstitious actions such as crossing fingers, touching wood or not stepping under ladders express the same desire for protection that drives religious ritual. Act in this way and you will be protected from some undefined, and as yet unrealised, calamity.

Why, in a scientific age, do such actions remain so attractive to so many? One answer might lie in the way in which such actions forge a connection between self and world. In daily life we frequently connect disparate and unconnected experiences. I go out without an umbrella and feel that the inevitable shower of rain is precisely that: inevitable. I think of someone and the next minute they are on the phone. My response to this conjunction of events is to think that my 'conjuring them up' in thought has 'made them' call me.

In *Totem and Taboo*, Freud argues that this kind of magical thinking reflects the experience of primitive humans. They had 'an immense belief in the power of [their] wishes' (Freud, 1913a: 83). Thought and world were intimately connected. Thoughts and words had the power to change things. This belief in 'the omnipotence of thought' mirrors the experience of children before they have adequately developed their ability to control their bodies' movements. Through the mother's response to their wishes, they develop a sense that their thoughts are all-powerful, capable of conjuring food and comfort 'out of nothing'. The infant's experience thus forms the bedrock for religion and superstition: that wishes and thoughts can change the world. In religion, this takes on a particular ritualistic shape, most notably in prayer, when thought connects the individual to the God in control of all things.

On one level it is relatively easy to dismiss such claims. There is no evidence for the kind of influence that the primitive, the child, and the religious believer associate with thought. Yet on an emotional level there is something very powerful and tenacious at work. An intimate connection is being assumed between the individual's thoughts, desires, and wishes and the wider cosmos. Given the threats posed by that external world, a degree of psychic reassurance can be attained through making that connection.

Interestingly, Freud provides examples of his actions that illustrate this desire to connect with the cosmos. In an addition to *The Psychopathology of Everyday Life* (1901) made in 1907, Freud tells of an incident following the restoration of his eldest daughter to health after a severe illness in 1905. Passing through his study, 'I yielded to a sudden impulse and hurled one of my slippers from my foot at the wall, causing a beautiful little marble Venus to fall down from its bracket' (Freud, 1901 [1907]: 169). As it breaks into pieces, Freud finds himself quoting, 'quite unmoved', a passage from Busch: 'Oh! The Venus! Lost is she!' Freud sees 'the wild conduct and my calm acceptance of the damage' thus:

> My attack of destructive fury served therefore to express a feeling of gratitude to fate and allowed me to perform a '*sacrificial act*' – rather as if I had made a vow to sacrifice something or other as a thank-offering if she recovered her health! (Freud, 1901 [1907]: 169)

On one level this action makes no sense at all. It is unnecessarily destructive. It achieves nothing. Freud reads it rather differently. It comes in the wake of his daughter's illness. She has recovered. This may reflect the medical expertise of her doctors; a purely rational response might be to pay them a bonus or give them a gift. But a different psychological response is required, which relates to the unconscious fears and desires of attending to a sick child. Having gone through a period of considerable anxiety, Freud feels the need to make 'a thank-offering' to a power, which here he calls 'fate', that lies outside the human realm of doctors and medical practice. We will pick up on the importance of fate in his thinking in a moment. His daughter has been spared and a cosmic force must be thanked. Hence his 'calm acceptance' of the damage his action brings.

This begs the question of whether Freud's hope that religion will disappear as the scientific revolution takes hold is realistic. What he seems to be getting at in the example of the Broken Venus is that there is something deeply entrenched in human beings that longs to make connections of this kind between self and world. The seventeenth-century mathematician and religious thinker Blaise Pascal described with great power the immensity of the cosmos in which humans find themselves. 'Through space the universe grasps me and swallows me up like a speck,' he wrote, capturing the terror that recognizing that experience of infinite space can have on the human heart. In the example of the Broken Venus, Freud displays the completely understandable impulse to connect with those cosmic forces that transcend the individual and can so easily destroy them. With the best will in the world, it is difficult to see how science could ever offer complete reassurance in the face of these powers. In which case, can the religious desire to connect ever be completely eradicated?

Freud's superstitious inclinations suggest something of the tenacity of that desire to connect with faceless cosmic powers. Freud was obsessed – as are many of us – with death, and particularly with the uncertainty of when his death would come. While some might be glad not to know, for others that lack of knowledge can be hard. Today, a resolution of sorts can be found in the 'Death Watch' app. You enter data about your health and lifestyle and it comes up with a projected death date. It helpfully provides a 'Death Watch', which counts down to that date. (Try it if you dare!) Writing before such gadgetry, Freud turned to numerology. At various points in his life he was convinced that he would die at the age of 51, 61, or 62, the last figure derived from the publication date of *The Interpretation of Dreams* and his telephone number. As Michael Palmer points out, he was also fascinated by ideas of clairvoyance and telepathy. It would seem that a commitment to science is not enough to drive out the impulses to make connections that go way beyond the careful methods of science.

How does this affect the reading of Freud on religion? While the main thrust of Freud's critique is to expose religion as a form of false belief about the nature of the world and our place in it, an equally important thread runs beneath his criticisms. The fears and desires that shape our earliest experience of the world and that continue to haunt us as we move into adulthood are just as significant for understanding human individuality and society as reason and conscious thought. Pursuing his ideas on these fears and desires suggests a different way of reading his account of religion.

Superstitious action and religious belief reflect what Freud describes as the need to 'feel at home in the uncanny' (Freud, 1927a: 17). When we speak of the uncanny, we usually have in mind things like ghosts and hauntings, *doppelgangers* (doubles), and *déjà vu*. Such experiences are perplexing and unsettling: the stuff of countless horror films. They are both unfamiliar and strange and yet they also have another quality to which Freud draws our attention. They may be strange but there is something about such stories and experiences that unsettle because they are not as unfamiliar as we might initially think.

The idea that the uncanny is something both familiar and strange is reflected rather well in German. As Freud notes, 'The German word [for the uncanny] "*unheimlich*" (unhomely) is obviously the opposite of "*heimlich*" (homely), "*heimisch*" (native) – the opposite of familiar'. While this might tempt us to conclude 'that what is "uncanny" is frightening precisely because it is not known and familiar' (Freud, 1919: 220), Freud rejects this view. What is '*unheimlich*' is frightening because it is actually all-too-familiar and known. For Freud, this paradoxical experience is significant, for it represents 'a return of the repressed'.

Think for a moment about the dynamic of ghost stories. In many ghost stories a spectre appears in order to expose something known by the central character that has long been forgotten. In the 2011 film *The Awakening*, a woman intent on debunking spiritualism is asked to investigate the haunting of a school. The ghost of a screaming boy has been seen. As the story unfolds, she is confronted with parts of her own forgotten past and comes to realize that the ghost boy who so terrifies her is a forgotten playmate from her past who was murdered by her father. The memory of the killing that she has repressed with so much force has returned in the haunting of the school.

What interests Freud when he uses this term is not so much stories of supposed paranormal activity but the dual quality of the experience to which this idea refers. Strachey's English translation of '*unheimlich*' as 'uncanny' is not altogether helpful for understanding what Freud is getting at. When Freud says that we need to find ways of feeling at home in the uncanny, a more literal rendition of the German might give us a better idea. How are we to feel 'at home in the *unhomely*'? By raising this question, Freud draws our attention to the human experience of not feeling wholly at home in the natural world. We both are and are not comfortable in our environment. For Freud, human beings expend considerable time finding ways of making themselves feel at home in this often frightening world. In religion we find a particularly powerful example of the attempt to make the world a safe place in which to live.

The other Freud: Freud and fate

Freud's concern is to show why religion fails to offer an appropriate solution to the problem of how to feel at home in the world.

But in rejecting the religious account, he offers his reader tantalizing glimpses of what a more appropriate philosophy of life might involve.

To use the term 'philosophy of life' is far from uncontroversial for an appraisal of Freud. For a start, it might well be argued that Freud never offers a philosophy of life: not least because he is extremely critical of all philosophical perspectives. His main criticism is that philosophy as a practice emanates from a melancholic disposition that is seeking to answer questions that could never be answered (E. Freud, 1960: 436). We might think of the question 'Why am I here?' or 'What is the meaning of life?' Any answer we offer is likely to be speculative; for Freud this means that it is fundamentally a waste of time. More than that, engaging in such philosophical speculations reflects a depressed attitude. Rather than chase unanswerable questions, a better – a healthier – response would be to replace fruitless philosophical inquiry with empirical scientific investigation (Freud, 1916–17: 20).

Freud could be accused of protesting too much. As William McGrath has shown, his early studies in philosophy, while a university student, shape the way he thinks about many things, including religion. McGrath notes his considerable interest in the ideas of the German philosopher Ludwig Feuerbach (1804–72) who argued that the concept of God is created by human beings; a projection that reflects the desires and values of the societies that they inhabit. A similar move can be discerned in Freud's criticisms of religious belief.

Even if we accept that Freud was interested in philosophy, that doesn't imply that he constructed a philosophy of life. Given that so much of Freud's clinical work is with people struggling to find a way through life, it would seem strange if he did not engage in some way with the question of how to live. In his reflections on the nature and goal of psychoanalytic therapy, there are indications of what that philosophy of life might be, even if others – Freud included – might shy away from identifying such an endeavour in his work. He may not offer a systematic set of proposals but he does offer reflections on how to live that reflect his opposition to religious claims, as well as offering a different way of engaging with the world.

These ideas are present from the start. At the end of the *Studies on Hysteria*, Freud reflects on what the psychotherapeutic treatment of hysteria might achieve. He personalizes this question by adopting the perspective of one of his patients. She has been shown, through her treatment, that her illness was connected to 'my circumstances and the events of my life' (Freud, 1893–5: 305). Given that the past events that have formed her responses cannot be changed, she asks Freud a vital question: 'How do you propose to help me?' (Freud, 1893–5: 305). Freud's response suggests something of the limits but also the possibilities of psychoanalytic therapy:

> No doubt fate would find it easier than I do to relieve you of your illness. But you will be able to convince yourself that much will be gained if we succeed in transforming your hysterical misery into common unhappiness. With a mental life that has been restored to health you will be better armed against that unhappiness (Freud, 1893–95: 305).

A subtle shift takes place in these words. Freud begins his practice as a medical physician; someone who trades in curing disease. What he recognizes as he develops his psychoanalytic practice are the limits of effecting a lasting cure for his patients when their troubles lie in the mind. To cure emotional and mental disease depends not only on the prowess of the doctor but also on factors which lie far outside the control of either analyst or patient. In this context, he introduces the idea of 'fate'. Events and experiences outside one's control shaped one's character in the first place. Psychoanalytic therapy cannot override the basic nature of the world but what it can do is strengthen the tools that ensure mental health or, as Nicola Luckhurst's recent translation puts it, one's 'inner life'.

The troubling issue of whether 'cure' is possible retains its hold, arising again in the late 1930s. Freud uses similar language to suggest a means of proceeding. His understanding of the task of analysis has moved into the realm of 'character analysis' (Freud, 1937a: 250). Analysis, understood in this way, seeks to shore up the fragile ego in the face of the onslaught of unconscious forces. Again, Freud is compelled to ask whether the work of analysis can ever be 'final'. Can the analyst really hope to have had such a 'far-reaching influence on the patient that no further change could be expected to take place in him if his analysis were continued' (Freud, 1937a: 219)?

Freud is unsure that such an outcome is possible, given that this would imply the possibility of attaining 'a level of absolute psychical normality' (Freud, 1937a: 219–20). He also notes, as he did in the 1880s, that the success of an analysis is dependent on two factors outside the analyst's control: 'the constitutional and the accidental' (Freud, 1937a: 220). In other words, lasting healing is dependent on those events and experiences that have formed our characters, as well as the things that happen to us. He turns to the language of fate to express what he is getting at:

> If the patient who has been restored in this way never produces another disorder calling for analysis, we do not know how much his immunity may not be due to *a kind fate* which has spared him ordeals that are too severe (Freud, 1937a: 220; my emphasis).

The appeal to fate sounds strange for a scientist but this is no mere linguistic quirk or literary flourish. An exploration of what is denoted by his use of fate throws light both on his rejection of religion and on his understanding of what makes for a fulfilling human life.

We have already come across one of the ways in which Freud employs the language of fate. In *The Future of an Illusion*, he uses fate to describe the external forces lying outside the protective structures of human civilization. Fate is connected explicitly with the terrors of Nature that the advent of civilization seeks to curtail. At times Freud appears to consign such fears to the past and the experience of primitive peoples: 'To this [the sufferings inflicted by society and other individuals] are added the injuries which untamed nature – *he calls it Fate* – inflicts on him' (Freud, 1927a: 16; my emphasis).

This is not to say that he relegates fate to the past; elsewhere he uses it to describe the more general human experience of the world. Through natural forces (floods, disease, and death), 'nature rises up against *us*, majestic, cruel and inexorable' (Freud, 1927a: 16; my emphasis): 'us' not 'them'. These features of the world act as reminders of the weakness of human beings, for civilization is not a panacea for all ills. There are, as Freud notes, 'the elements, which seem to mock all human control' (Freud, 1927a: 15).

Against this backdrop, Freud accepts the psychological efficacy of religion as a means of responding to the unpredictable nature of fate. Through the creation of gods who 'reconcile men to the cruelty of Fate' (Freud, 1927a: 18), people are able to believe that they can manipulate fate; although these forms of manipulation are illusory, not based in fact.

Freud's response – the 'mature' response – is different. His is a position beyond religion. He argues 'for the renunciation of wishes and for acquiescence in Fate' (Freud, 1927a: 36). Belief in God or gods must be renounced, along with the wishful attempt to influence the external world. One has to accept fate. The effect of this position is stark for those who adopt it but it is the only option open to mature human beings:

> They can no longer be the centre of creation, no longer the object of tender care on the part of a beneficent Providence.

They will be in the same position as a child who has left the parental house where he was so warm and comfortable. But surely infantilism is destined to be surmounted. Men cannot remain children for ever; they must in the end go out into 'hostile life' (Freud, 1927a: 49).

The tension between Freud the scientific optimist and the Freud who is more pessimistic about the possibilities of progress is evident here. 'Infantilism is destined to be surmounted'; the end of religion is therefore inevitable. Human ingenuity can improve much in human life; science can contribute to the progress of humanity. At the same time he insists that life remains hostile; parts of human experience continue to be untouched by scientific progress for they are ultimately beyond human influence and manipulation. Confronted with the experiences of mortality – suffering, decay, death – only one response is possible: 'As for the great necessities of Fate, against which there is no help, they will learn to endure them with resignation' (Freud, 1927a: 50).

Resigning oneself to the realities of a particular situation is no easy thing to do. It is the struggle to accept fate that is alluded to by Freud's patient from the *Studies on Hysteria*. Her difficulty stems from two interlocking concerns: how to accept 'the way things are' (in other words, the circumstances that have defined her character) and 'the way things go' (those external events lying outside human control). The issue becomes how to get on with life. Freud is well aware of the powerful temptation of using ritual as a means of exercising an illusory sense of control over life's uncertainties. If *The Future of an Illusion* notes the childishness of such attempts, he is not always so dismissive. Confronted with the vicissitudes of fate, with human powerlessness, the desire 'to sacrifice something to Fate in order to ward off some other dreaded loss' (Freud, 1916–17: 77) is perfectly natural. Remember Freud's sacrifice of the 'little Venus'. Such 'sacrifices' provide a way to 'exorcise Fate' (Freud, 1916–17: 77), reflecting the desire to find a way of moving beyond the hold that fate has over our lives.

Fate is never neutral. In the example of the Broken Venus, Freud tells the experience of a 'kind' fate: his daughter Mathilde had recovered from her illness. The death of his beloved daughter Sophie, in 1920, revealed another possible outcome to illness. Freud writes wearily to Lajos Levy: 'to outlive a child is not agreeable. Fate does not keep even to this order of precedence'. These deeply personal examples suggest something of the uncertainty of the world in which we find ourselves. Nothing can be taken for granted; it is precisely this uncertainty that affects what psychoanalysis may or may not be able to achieve.

Accepting fate: Stoicism and psychoanalytic practice

Accepting the uncertainty of life, while resisting the pull of religious solutions, does not mean that Freud has no suggestions for living. In psychoanalysis, a powerful tool is offered for addressing the pains and ills of life. At the end of the *Studies on Hysteria* he suggests that the work of psychoanalysis is to strengthen the patient's '*Seelenleben*'. While this might be translated as one's mental life, Bruno Bettelheim argues that it is best translated literally, as 'the life of the soul'. Understanding *Seelenleben* in this way resists an account of analysis as simply an intellectual process for cultivating detachment. As Bettelheim points out, analysis involves integrating one's emotional and intellectual life and thus has more in common with religious strategies than we might initially think. The question is how to achieve wholeness rather than simply the strengthening of mental capabilities.

Freud's character suggests connections with other historical attempts to cultivate such a way of living. Peter Gay finds parallels with one ancient philosophical school, describing Freud as 'an old Stoic'. While Gay might use this term loosely, to denote Freud's bravery in the face of adversity, it is worth exploring this connection in more depth, not least because it illuminates aspects of psychoanalytic practice that illuminate Freud's own beliefs about how best to live.

In his discussion of philosophy as a way of life, the French philosopher Pierre Hadot draws attention to 'the spiritual exercises' practiced by Stoic philosophers. He argues that the Hellenistic schools of late antiquity defined philosophy as a form of therapy for combating the ills of life. Their central concern was to establish what made for a happy life, though in practice what they meant by 'happiness' was not an emotional feeling but a fulfilling or contented way of living. Importantly for our purposes, the Stoic proposal for living differed radically to that of the religious. Rather than seek to manipulate fate (the things that happen) through ritual and worship of the gods, the Stoics focused their attention on identifying the things that could and could not be changed. Accepting the limits of human life enabled identification of those aspects of life over which a person had some degree of control. Ultimately, they identified the mind as the one thing over which an individual had power. As a result, it mattered less what happened to a person but more how they responded to events. Cultivating reason became a vital way of engaging with the world, for only reason could challenge a purely emotional response to events.

The emphasis placed by the Stoics on the rational self makes it difficult to sustain a straightforward parallel between Freud's ideas and theirs but there are some similarities. Like Freud, the Stoics place limits upon the extent to which the external world can be manipulated or shaped by human beings. In rejecting the religious attempt to influence the world through ritual, the Stoics put forward a radical solution to the ills of existence: if a person is to live contentedly, they have to accept the kind of universe in which they find themselves and adapt their wishes and attitudes accordingly. Assuming that the processes of the world have been established to cultivate human happiness, or that it can be forced to conform to our wishes, is a mistake that will lead only to disappointment and discontent. Freud agrees: 'One feels inclined to say that the intention that man should be "happy" is not included in the plan of "Creation"' (Freud, 1930: 77). A better strategy is to find ways of accepting how things actually are.

At this point, the parallels between Freud and the Stoics become most evident. The purpose of the spiritual exercise and the work of psychoanalytic reflection are remarkably similar. The Stoics placed great importance on 'attention' (*prosoche*). Establishing a form of dialogue with oneself was vital to cultivate a form of objective reflection towards one's life. This involved adopting a particular form of daily practice. In the morning, attention would be paid to the events of the day and how one's principles might be applied to the things that might happen. In the evening, the day's proceedings would be replayed, consideration being given to what faults might have been committed or what progress might have been made. Reflecting in this way on one's life also involved analysing one's dreams.

This connection between Freud and an ancient school of thought should not surprise us, given his interest in this period of human civilization. That is not to deny the differences between ancient Stoic practice and psychoanalysis. For the Stoic, the process of reflection is reasonably straightforward: there is little sense that unconscious motivations might drive a person's actions. Yet emphasising the importance of reflecting objectively on one's life and feelings resonates with Freud's ideas about the work of analysis. Developing critical reflection is central to the emphasis Freud later places on cultivating the ego. Through analysis, through subjecting dreams, emotions, and attitudes to critical reflection, the patient's mental resources can be strengthened. Through strengthening the rational, conscious self, it is possible to address the effect of early attachments and experiences on behaviour.

In the context of these reflections on the role of therapy we find another way in which Freud uses fate. It is also used to denote not the terrors of the natural world but the rule of 'destiny', the sense that one's life is in thrall to powers beyond the self that have determined the path it will follow. Analysis offers the possibility of challenging the perception that things are beyond one's control. Through analysis, the ego 'which has attained greater maturity and strength, [is able] to undertake a revision of these old repressions' (Freud, 1937a: 227). As Freud's colleague Richard Sterba notes, analysis strengthens the activity of the ego so that the subject's consciousness shifts from the turmoil of the emotions to intellectual contemplation of those emotions. Through this reflective process, what is unconscious becomes conscious. The patient no longer has to 'act out' the things that are troubling them, often at great cost to their relationships and life in the world. Instead, they are able to put those emotions into words, thereby achieving some kind of control over them.

Cultivating this sense of objectivity towards one's emotions and experiences is an important part of analytic practice because it challenges the idea that one has no choice, that one's experiences are 'fated' or 'destined'. Through working together, analyst and patient establish an alliance that helps free the patient from the harmful identifications and attitudes of the past. Reflection becomes possible as the patient cultivates 'some degree of aloofness' (Freud, 1920: 19) from their experience. This makes new ways of living possible. It is possible to consider one's emotions, experiences, feelings of shame or guilt in ways that do not lead automatically to the implementation of defensive strategies to limit the pain of that engagement. Eventually, through modelling the work of analysis in their daily life, the patient develops the critical tools to do this work themselves; they become an analyst for themselves. As a result, the ability of the past to shape current experience becomes something which can be challenged. The hold of fate, in this sense, can be broken.

Establishing this reflective attitude involves instigating an internal dialogue. Here Freud's practice and that of the Stoics coincide. Through analysis, it is possible to come to a clearer sense of one's self. Note the importance of relationship: analysis does not seek to cultivate self-absorption. Dialogue in the self is based on a relationship with another who listens. The relationship between analyst and patient thus provides the model for reflective practice and for other relationships.

We might note parallels with the experience of the confessional here. The priest, like the analyst, models a form of reflective conversation that is then internalized in the mind of the one confessing. This analogy should not be pushed too far: there are clearly differences in the goals of these conversations. But common to both is the development of a reflective attitude, where one's life becomes something that can be considered apart from one's immediate experience of it. To adopt Bettelheim's translation, through developing 'the life of the soul', a deeper understanding of one's self emerges, which enables better relationships with others and the world. There may be more common ground between aspects of the religious or spiritual life and the work of psychoanalysis than Freud would care to admit.

Accepting transience

And so we find ourselves back at the question of religion. This might seem strange, given that Freud is undoubtedly extremely critical of religion. But we might want to probe a little more deeply into what kind of religion he has in his sights. He is clearly troubled by religions that misrepresent the nature of reality. When he attacks religious beliefs, he connects them explicitly to an illusory supernatural realm that acts to fulfil infantile wishes.

Critics have argued that aiming his fire at one kind of religion severely limits the success of his critique. Not all religious perspectives can be characterized in this way, for example, religions like Buddhism are not shaped by the figure of a supernatural father-god.

Perhaps there is a different way of exploring what he says. Reading his critique of religion alongside his discussion of how to engage with fate suggests some common concerns with those who seek to reflect on the nature of reality and who use religious ideas as a framework for this enterprise. Freud's psychoanalytic practice, understood as a means of promoting the reflective inner life in order to live differently, shares a commitment to 'mindfulness' that defines the spiritual practices of many religious traditions.

Such a reading might challenge the idea that Freud has no place or sympathy for religion. There is clearly something about religion that fascinates Freud, even if he delights in calling himself a 'Godless Jew'. His last work, *Moses and Monotheism* (1939), finds him grappling with the question of Jewish identity, albeit in a way that horrified his Jewish contemporaries. In this work, he challenges the idea that Moses was a Hebrew, arguing instead that the Moses who gives the Israelites the Ten Commandments is an Egyptian, a follower of the radical monotheist Pharaoh Akhenaten (died around 1336 BCE). This is a controversial reading, to say the least, and reflects his complex relationship with his Jewish inheritance. Throughout his time in Vienna he was a member of the B'nai B'rith, a Jewish society. He was also fascinated by the figure of Moses, and wrote of the effect Michelangelo's statue of the patriarch, which he visited on a number of occasions, had on him (Freud, 1914c).

Jewish identity can take either a religious or secular form. Freud was proud of his Jewish inheritance, if not its religious form. But even accepting that distinction, his attitude to religious belief is far more complex than might be suggested if one were only to read *The Future of an Illusion, Totem and Taboo,* and *Civilisation and Its Discontents.*

According to the contemporary psychoanalyst Salman Akhtar, the imaginary believer of *The Future of Illusion*, with whom Freud debates, represents an aspect of Freud. For Akhtar, '"Freud the Atheist" is in bloody combat with "Freud the Believer"!' (Akhtar in O'Neil and Akhtar, 2009: 3). This comment may overplay the distinction between these 'two Freuds'. The informal correspondence between Freud and his friends Oskar Pfister and Romain Rolland, who were both religious believers, suggests a willingness to talk more respectfully of the religious perspective. Pfister was disappointed that this subtlety was not reflected in the tone of *The Future of an Illusion*. As he puts it in a letter from February 1928: 'You are much better and deeper than your disbelief' (Meng and E. Freud, 1963: 122).

There is one short but beautiful paper that suggests something of the Freud who is less rigid about diverting into the territory traditionally occupied by the religious. In 'On Transience', written in 1915, Freud gives an indication of how acceptance of the passing nature of the world might lead not to tragic introspection but to a renewed engagement with the beauty of this world. The position he outlines stands as a counterpoint to perspectives that seek to render the universe either too meaningful or completely meaningless.

Freud describes 'a summer walk through a smiling countryside' in the company of two friends, one a poet, the other a 'taciturn' friend. Matthew von Unwerth identifies these companions as the poet Rainer Maria Rilke and Freud's firm friend Lou Andreas-Salomé. The poet is in a dark mood and finds in the beauty of the countryside little cause for celebration: 'all this beauty was fated to extinction ... it would vanish when winter came, like all human beauty and all the beauty and splendour that men have created or may create' (Freud, 1916 [1915]: 305).

Freud takes the identification of this state of affairs as his starting point. There are, he comments, two possible responses identified in his companions' attitudes to the transient beauty of the world. The first is the 'aching despondency' of the young poet, which leads to a sense that life is tragic and without meaning. Depression and pessimism seem inevitable if one accepts that the universe is such that all is in flux, all is passing away. The second response is rather different: a kind of 'rebellion' arises in the breast of the observer, which lends itself all too readily to the belief in immortality. This second response refuses to accept that such loveliness can ever really die; thus the observer looks to an eternal realm to support the idea that far from ephemeral, beauty in its 'true' form is indestructible.

Here we are presented with the contrast between what Freud takes to be the non-religious and the religious views of the world. Can an alternative perspective be found? The refusal to accept transience and the postulation of an eternal realm is dismissed, not surprisingly, for being based on futile wishes. Just because you wish for such an eternal realm does not make it so. Resisting the reality of transience reveals the disposition of the religious mindset that clings to infantile illusions and seeks solace in childish wish-fulfilments.

Must we join the poet in his depressing evaluation of this world's beauty? This is where things become interesting, for Freud suggests another way forward, in which, as he puts it: 'transience value is scarcity value in time' (Freud, 1916 [1915]: 305). In other words, beauty is valued precisely because we know it is passing. Its fragility and contingency makes it something rare and because it is rare, we value it all the more highly. The vulnerability and fragility of the beauty of this world does not make it less valuable but all the more valuable. As he poetically puts it, 'a flower that blossoms only for a single night does not seem to us on that account less lovely' (Freud, 1916 [1915]: 306). One must learn to accept the ephemeral nature of things without regret and by so doing one is able to place one's own life in the context of a changing but beautiful world. Rather than resist such a view of one's life, it will be possible to accept it. Achieving acceptance will take considerable effort, and requires the cultivation of a particular kind of reflection, but Freud holds it out to us as a possibility to be pursued and practiced.

Freud may reject the metaphysical tendencies of the religious, categorized as the futile attempt to give the universe a friendly human face. Yet that does not mean that he sees the world as lacking meaning or without beauty. Through the process of psychoanalysis it is possible to ground a sense of life as something meaningful, finding in its wake activities and ways of living that give shape to life's apparently random nature. We come to recognize the experiences and events that have created us, the power of the unconscious to influence our actions, and the possibility that by cultivating a more reflective mindset we might make new things happen in our lives. We need not be stuck in the past, unable to be fully alive in the present.

At the same time, this critical reflection involves placing one's life in the broader movements of the cosmos. Accepting that life is fragile, fleet, and subject to luck and chance need not mean that it is without meaning or incapable of being lived to the full. Recognizing that all is passing gives impetus to the need to shape lives that are worth living.

In providing the tools for shaping a form of reflective practice relevant to the contemporary world, Freud founds a discipline that enables the development of a meaningful life, in which the unpredictability of life is not evaded, but accepted. His critique of religion need not lead to hopelessness and the end of meaning. Indeed, in challenging the false science of some religious claims he opens up the possibility of grounding religious reflection and spiritual practice in the processes and movements of a transient yet beautiful universe.

6
Freud in the twenty-first century

The previous chapter concluded with some suggestions about how we might read Freud on religion. Those reflections might well have been disputed by Freud but they stem from reading his critique of religion alongside other themes in his writings, in which he reflects on the nature of the world and human beings' place in it.

New readings of Freud are far from uncommon and suggest something of the richness of his work. The breadth and depth of his writing makes him an enthralling conversation partner for his readers. Psychoanalysis today might have 'moved on' from his original theories, his ideas are now largely communicated through the theories of those psychoanalysts who followed him. But this does not mean that he has nothing to offer the question of how to make sense of our lives. His continued relevance can, I think, be traced to the sheer scope of his enquiry. Freud does not confine himself to analysing one aspect of human experience; all is present in his writing, from the seemingly most trivial to the most profound. Nor does he confine himself rigidly to one method: scientific practice, clinical observation, philosophical and historical speculation, and literary and artistic criticism shape and influence the way in which he comes to his conclusions about what it is to be human. Because of this, readers may well find that some works speak more powerfully to them than others, enabling new perspectives to develop, informed by the issues that most concern that reader.

At the same time, the evolving nature of his work contributes to the sense that the reader is accompanying him on his intellectual journey. He is an innovator who builds on ideas that precede him, while finding it necessary to create his own language for the phenomena he encounters in his clinical practice. To read him is to discover someone attempting to create a new way of approaching the human subject. The way is by no means easy and at times he has to refine his ideas significantly. Because of this, his readers are far from passive observers and there is no obvious or straightforward way of reading him.

We have seen something of the variety of readings possible, in exploring the difference between British and French psychoanalysis. Emphasizing the importance of different texts for understanding Freud shapes the way in which those psychoanalytic traditions continue to evolve. Freud's ideas form a starting point for reflection, rather than a final resting place. As we conclude this book, it is worth spending some time thinking about the way in which Freud might speak to us, our lives, and our times. The two suggestions for possible readings that follow are by no means exhaustive. Everyone has to encounter Freud for themselves and come to their own view of what speaks most to them. However, these two visions of Freud might readily resonate with the concerns of his early-twenty-first-century readers.

Freud the cultural critic

This is the Freud who challenges the assumptions and attitudes of his day and who challenges us, in turn, to look critically at our own times.

The area of Freud's thought that most challenged his contemporaries was his claim that sexuality was central to understanding what it is to be human. It is tempting to think that contemporary liberal, Western societies have accepted that claim.

Popular culture suggests an easy acceptance of sexuality. Magazines proclaim a healthy sex life as important for self-fulfilment. Businesses recognize that 'sex sells' and, in their advertising, explicitly seek to address the desires that frame our purchasing power.

This apparent acceptance of Freud's desiring subject masks an unwillingness to accept the more controversial elements of Freud's analysis. If we follow Freud's advice to go beneath the surface of behaviours and attitudes, we find modern free-thinking about sex is far from comfortable with the implications of Freud's claim that sexual desire permeates all aspects of human experience.

This is most obvious in the central place that Freud gives to the Oedipus complex. The claim that children are sexual beings with a rich phantasy life remains as shocking now as it was at the beginning of the twentieth century. The common belief that children are 'innocent' of sexuality and sexual feelings ignores the extent to which they seek to understand the mysterious realm of sexuality. Remember that Freud's account of what constitutes 'the sexual' moves us far beyond limiting that concept to genital pleasure. 'The sexual' encompasses both physical and psychical experiences. Denying that this is the case neglects the frequently messy and sometimes distressing exploration of sex in the lives of children and adolescents.

For many, Freud's rejection of sexual abuse as the root cause of hysteria remains the barrier that stops them accepting his psychosexual theory. As we have seen, he came to this conclusion not because he denied abuse ever took place but because he wished to draw attention to the powerful phantasies of parental seduction that drove such illnesses. Does this shift in emphasis away from 'the real world' to that of the unconscious and desire make him a denier of sexual abuse? Not necessarily. By emphasizing the phantasies that shape our engagement with the world he offers a tool for considering afresh the destructive impact of abusive relationships.

Freud refuses to reduce sexuality to specific sexual acts. Sex is never simply confined to the experiences of the physical body. It is also constructed through the phantasies which emerge from the individual circumstances of our infancies. Against this back-drop, child abuse is horrific not just because of the actions of the abuser that take place in the 'real' world of the physical. When abuse takes place, the desires of the child – those phantastical constructions that are not part of that physical world – are brought into reality, often with extremely damaging consequences.

Vladimir Nabokov's *Lolita* provides a window into the com-plex layers that can make up an abusive relationship. Towards the end of the book, Humbert looks back on his life with Lolita, the twelve-year-old 'nymphet' whom he has abducted and seduced. Lolita is Humbert's step-daughter who, before the abduction, had a girlish crush on her step-father. This has been made real because of Humbert's actions. The story is told from Humbert's perspec-tive; the wit of Nabokov's writing seduces the reader into accept-ing his view of their relationship. But there is a sickening moment towards the end of the book that brings the reader up sharply, reminding us of what has happened to this girl:

> There was the day when having withdrawn the functional promise I had made her on the eve (whatever she had set her funny little heart on – a roller rink with some special plastic floor or a movie matinée to which she wanted to go alone), I happened to glimpse from the bathroom, through a chance combination of mirror aslant and door ajar, a look on her face … that look I cannot exactly describe … an expression of help-lessness so perfect that it seemed to grade into one of rather comfortable inanity just because this was the very limit of injus-tice and frustration – and every limit presupposes something beyond it – hence the natural illumination. And when you bear in mind that these were the raised eyebrows and parted lips of a child, you may better appreciate what depths of calculated

carnality, what reflected despair, restrained me from falling at her
dear feet and dissolving in human tears ...

In that small moment, Nabokov opens a window on to Lolita's
experience. She is a child, who should be enjoying the things of
girlhood. Her thoughts about sex should be part of her imaginary world. Instead, she is confined to various hotel bedrooms,
isolated from other people, and in an all-consuming and manipu-
lative relationship with the man who should be acting as her
father. Having what Freud would call her 'Oedipal desires' to
displace the mother as the father's love-object actualized in this
way adds to the pain of her experience. By exploiting such phantasies, Humbert has trapped her in a world of his making.
Arguably, the full horror of this story can only be grasped if we
note, with Freud, the complex nature of sexuality, which com-
bines physical acts and the realm of phantasy (both unconscious
and conscious). Far from denying the horror of abuse, Freud's
ideas enable deeper reflection on the damage wrought by such
actions, as well as posing a challenge to some of the powerful
social narratives about childhood and choice. Such narratives are
not always helpful for understanding the complex nature of abusive relationships and the sexual exploitation of children by adults.

Pursuing the Freud who acts as cultural critic can lead to
other surprising conclusions. Freud was at pains to present himself as a 'Scientist of the Mind' who wanted to create a discipline
that accurately described the processes of the mind. Not surprisingly, this has led contemporary commentators such as Mark
Solms to claim that if Freud were alive today, he would have
joyfully embraced neuroscience and its success in mapping the
activity of the brain.

There is much to recommend this adoption of Freud by neuroscience. Freud was often embarrassed by the rather messy and
individualistic sources for his theory and would no doubt have
found the detached, objective style of neuroscience appealing.

Yet before Freud is claimed too quickly for neuroscience, it is important to note its limits for the kind of enterprise on which he embarked. The psychologist William Uttal describes neuroscience, in none-too-flattering terms, as the 'new phrenology'. The 'old' phrenologists of the nineteenth century, using measurements of the human skull, sought to identify particular psychological functions with particular areas of the brain, paving the way for the focus of contemporary neuroscientists. By drawing this parallel, Uttal intends to show the problems that arise from an over-extension of the interpretative scope of this method. Phrenologists, for example, thought they could identify criminality by measuring the skull. In emphasising the importance of locating psychological functions in particular parts of the brain, is the extension of neuroscientific findings to all aspects of life ignoring the importance of psychological studies of how individuals actually behave?

In the light of Uttal's critique, let us return to Freud. Freud's practice and theory goes well beyond the idea that it is only necessary to find a method of describing the processes of the human brain as accurately as possible. Freud's interest also lies in exploring human behaviour and relationships. Moreover, because his work evolves from his medical practice, he is never offering only a piece of pure scientific research. There is always the therapeutic element. He is a medical practitioner seeking to combat sickness. His clinical work aims at enabling more effective ways of living for those whose lives are blighted by mental illness. This affects his scientific conclusions. Grounded in the lives of his patients, his theory offers a personalized engagement with the lived experience of being human, going beyond abstract description. It is personal, and always with a therapeutic aim directed at the individual's behaviour and attitudes. Alongside theorizing the workings of the mind, he seeks to develop methods that enable the troubled to come to terms with who they are and the things that they do.

This therapeutic focus, and what it entails in practice, moves us towards a second way of reading Freud that speaks powerfully to our times.

Freud the moral philosopher

At the end of the previous chapter we considered the possibility of a more creative relationship between Freud and the study of religion. There, we reflected on the possibility that certain forms of religion and Freud's ideas on fate might offer ways of coming to terms with life in a changing world. This connection requires us to think about the question of how to live. If we are uncomfortable with seeing Freud as offering a religious perspective that goes beyond the narrow theism that forms the focus of his critique, we might think instead about the contribution Freud makes as moral philosopher.

To call Freud a moral philosopher is almost as controversial as to call him religious. Freud would not have been happy about adopting this title. Yet the philosopher Alfred Tauber argues that it might be possible to think of Freud as a 'reluctant philosopher'. Attracted to philosophy as a young student, Freud rapidly became dissatisfied with the abstractions and generalizations of philosophical enquiry. Damning comments about the inadequacy of philosophical method pepper his work from start to finish.

This ostensible rejection masks the fact that Freud was never entirely able to resist the pull of the philosophical. In part, this comes from the necessary tension between his commitment to scientific method and the needs of the therapeutic. As soon as you attempt to find solutions to that which ails the human spirit, you cannot avoid raising the question of how human beings might live better and more fulfilling lives. For this reason, Freud cannot avoid philosophy. Specifically, he cannot avoid the branch of philosophy that moves the discipline from the realms of the abstract into the ethical dimension. It is important not to misunderstand what it means to talk about 'the ethical'. Rather than limiting this term to discussion of specific questions of what is right and what is wrong, it is best broadened as the subject which engages with the question of how to live.

Freud's therapeutic method leads him to the ground traditionally occupied by moral philosophy. As a therapist, his approach sits well with the description of philosophy, offered by the ancient philosopher Epicurus, as that which soothes the sick soul. To do this effectively, the philosopher/therapist must provide reflections that enable the individual to find the best way of living in the world. There is no easy answer to the question of what this means: especially if, like Freud (and Epicurus), you reject the certainties of religion.

The tools provided by psychoanalysis enable the strengthening of one's mental life, a process that makes possible more fulfilling ways of living. For Freud, these tools enable 'love and work' (Freud, 1930 [1929]: 101), the two features he identifies at the heart of a well-lived life. The combination of attaining mental clarity and then being able to enter into relationships and meaningful activity requires a further dimension. This links his clinical aims with his metapsychological speculations. To live well, one must find a way of orientating oneself with the rest of the universe.

When Freud extends his theories from explaining mental illness to more general statements about human activity, he does so by reiterating his claim that human life comprises both instinctual and mental attributes. This combination gives rise to the tragedy of the human condition, for there is a tension at the heart of the human animal. Freud the biologist recognizes that humans are animals driven by their instincts, including the sexual instincts. Freud the psychologist notes that humans are not simply located in that animal world. They are animals but of a peculiar kind. Instinctual desires to reproduce or kill can be sublimated into the energy that brings forth great art, philosophy, and literature. While this brings about the treasures of human culture, it also means that we are never entirely satisfied. To attain the protection offered by living in a community, we have to sublimate the desires that would otherwise destroy it.

This psychoanalytic theory of human culture cannot avoid becoming philosophical in tone. Freud's therapeutic method aims at making that which is unconscious, conscious. With this new-found clarity, the patient can again find their place in the world. To live well, the individual must find a means of locating their desires and needs in the wider context of the universe in which they find themselves. Rather than misrepresent the nature of that universe – Freud's main criticism of religion – they must accept the universe as it is.

Freud's account of what this universe is like goes some way to undermining his overly optimistic belief in the possibilities of science in a world that has rejected religious superstitions. Freud's cheerful, scientific optimism is never maintained; as the political philosopher Joshua Foa Dienstag points out, his view might best be described as a form of metaphysical pessimism. Freud sees the universe as one in which human beings are fated to endure a life wrought with problems that can never entirely be eradicated. He might play with the possibility – derived from the zoologist August Weismann (1834–1914) – that death 'cannot be regarded as an absolute necessity with its basis in the very nature of life' (Freud, 1920: 46) but ultimately he recognizes that it is not possible to change the fundamental context of human life. There is suffering and there is death. The human task is to find ways of living with those experiences and with that knowledge. Psychoanalysis is effective because it provides tools that strengthen the individual's mental life in the face of the sufferings of the world.

Locating his account of how to live against the backdrop of the dark realities of human experience challenges a dominant cultural narrative of contemporary Western societies. Since the

1990s, Western governments have struggled to understand why rising levels of affluence in the Western world have not been matched by a similar rise in levels of happiness. To address this apparent mismatch, educational strategies and social policies have been devised to cultivate and sustain elusive feelings of happiness.

The global financial crisis of 2008 has been heralded as marking the start of a new 'Age of Austerity', as governments across the world seek to cut public spending and reduce budget deficits. Despite such grim realities that invariably affect living standards, cultivating well-being remains a key concern for public policy. Rather than detail such initiatives, it is worth considering the cultural assumptions that dominate the concern with well-being, for here Freud proves a useful counterpoint to some popular narratives about what it means to live well.

A cursory glance at magazines, newspapers, and chat shows reveals a particular vision of 'the successful life'. To be successful, you should be happy; attractive; in a good, well-paid job in which you achieve status and respect; and in a good relationship that has produced beautiful children. To lose, or to lack, one of these elements is to run the risk of being seen as a 'failure'. And failure is something to be avoided at all costs. Against such a vision, there seems little place for the experiences of loss, suffering, or unhappiness.

Freud offers a contrasting view, which can come as something of a relief in the face of such an unremittingly upbeat vision of the successful life. He resolutely resists the assumption that life could be happy in the way such narratives suggest. Caught between the worlds of the instincts that demand satisfaction and the necessity of sublimating those instincts so that society can survive, happiness is not really an option. The twenty-first century belief that happiness can be achieved – whether through the freedom of the democratic process, by increasing our purchasing power, by becoming famous, or by resorting to a beautiful image constructed by a plastic surgeon – flies in the face of reality. Popular forms of psychotherapy maintain this myth by suggesting that happiness can be achieved if only you work hard enough on yourself. Therapy, in this account, becomes a way of achieving what you want that reflects the liberal hope of development and progress.

Freud's vision is precisely the opposite, because he recognizes the precarious nature of the human situation. Aligning one's expectations with the way the world is allows for a more realistic attitude to the goods that can be found in life. During a conversation with his friend and confidante Princess Marie Bonaparte, Freud reiterates the comments he made in his essay 'On Transience'. The Princess observes that she finds the passing of all things in the universe sad. Freud's response is to ask her 'Why sad? It is the way of life. It is precisely its eternal flow that makes it beautiful.' Recognizing the flux of life and your place in a changing, mutable universe makes possible a different way of engaging with life's suffering. If you like, it puts things in an eternal perspective by placing one's concerns against the backdrop of the immensity of the universe, the longevity of its history and the power of its processes. Our suffering ceases to be directed personally at us by a malicious Nature or God and becomes, instead, part of the way the world is.

To adopt this perspective does not mean that Freud downplays the fundamentally tragic nature of life. There is no fake joy or easy acceptance to be had in such a view. This was played out in his own life: close to death and experiencing terrible pain from the cancer in his jaw, Freud recognized that this was the end and chose to bring his own life to a close. Freud's reasons were that the pain he was suffering meant he had lost any sense of life's meaning: 'now all is torture and it has no more sense'. All come eventually to death's door; while this means there can be no truly happy endings, it does not mean that the path of life that brought us to this point need be meaningless.

The tools of psychotherapy become significant here, offering, as Dienstag notes, a method for managing the human condition.

This rather modest approach takes account of the cosmic backdrop. It is on cultivating 'techniques of living' – ways of coming to an accommodation with the struggles of life – that Freud places his emphasis. He offers no easy answers about how to live, for there are no obvious appeals that can be made to higher powers or authorities. What he offers is a realistic way of engaging with the frequently painful and messy experiences of our lives, through the process of psychoanalytic reflection. Engaging seriously and honestly with our lives provides tools to shape a life that can be meaningful even in the face of suffering and death. Like the ancient Stoic philosophers, Freud helps us to think about the nature of our lives by locating our experiences in the broader universe.

This is an exacting route to take and necessitates putting aside the illusion that there might be an easy path through life, if only we could find it. But the limited solutions that Freud offers have a certain kind of richness. He encourages us to see the world and ourselves differently; he offers us, if you like, new eyes with which to observe the all-too-familiar. He makes strange that which we think of as 'normal', while connecting this all-too-comfortable category with the apparently 'abnormal' behaviours of problematic 'others'. He disorientates our sense of who we are and changes the way in which we subsequently reflect on the world, ourselves, and each other. In this sense, his work is analogous to that of great artists. He helps us to see the world differently and the vision he presents is full of more colour and life than we might previously have imagined. He enables us to look at the things of this world differently, transforming our appreciation of the mundane. Challenging us to look again at that which we take for granted, the 'ordinary' is transformed.

At the heart of this new perception is Freud's account of the self. Never transparent, always opaque, the work of self-knowledge – the famous directive of the Delphic Oracle – involves considerable work. So much so that it might better be described as the work of self-creation. Only by interrogating our motivations, our assumptions, and our habitual ways of thinking about our lives can this mysterious 'I' emerge from the shadows. Through facing ourselves (our desires, wishes, fears, and anxieties) we can begin to live more creatively. Far from being anachronistic and irrelevant, Freud's ideas provide ways of thinking again about our experiences and his practices enable new ways of thinking and living to emerge. This is what makes him such a colossal intellectual figure so many years after his death. It is not just that his writing reveals him to be one of the greatest thinkers and innovators of the modern age; it is that through entering into dialogue with him, new light can be cast on what it means to be alive and – most importantly – what it means to really live.

Suggestions for further reading

Chapter 1

For the best recent introduction to Freud's work by a writer who is both a psychoanalyst and a philosopher, see Jonathan Lear's *Freud* (London: Routledge, 2005). For a useful dictionary of psychoanalytic terms, see Jean Laplanche and Jean-Bertrand Pontalis, *The Language of Psychoanalysis* (London: Karnac, 1988).

Peter Gay's fascinating biography, *Freud: A Life for Our Time* (Macmillan: Papermac, 1995) remains the best account of his life and work. For the perspective of one of his followers, see Ernest Jones's *The Life and Work of Sigmund Freud*, edited and abridged by L. Trilling and S. Marcus (New York: Basic Books, 1961). For an account of the last years of Freud's life, which intersects his story with that of Hitler and the rise of the Nazis, see Mark Edmundson's *The Death of Sigmund Freud* (London: Bloomsbury, 2007). For a compelling cultural history of the creation of psychoanalysis, see George Makari's *Revolution in Mind* (New York: HarperCollins, 2010). The comments on the loss of Sophie and Heinele come from Gay pp. 391–2 and p. 422 respectively. His comments that at least the Nazis are only burning books come from Gay pp. 592–3.

Freud remains a controversial figure, who elicits hero-worship on the part of some, loathing on the part of others. Janet Malcolm's *In the Freud Archives* (London: Fontana, 1984) provides a readable account of the controversy surrounding Freud's archive, including critical assessments made of him and his work by Jeffrey Masson and Peter Swales. A more recent but equally critical appraisal is given by Richard Webster in *Why Freud Was Wrong* (London: HarperCollins, 1995). Whatever the facts of the matter, Freud was evidently an imposing figure who left a powerful impression upon his patients. Sergei Pankejeff (who appears in the case studies as 'the Wolf Man') describes Freud thus:

> Freud's appearance was such as to win my confidence immediately. He was then in his middle fifties and seemed to enjoy the best of health. He was of medium height and figure. In his rather long face, framed by a closely-clipped, already greying beard, the most impressive feature was his intelligent dark eyes, which looked at me penetratingly but without causing me the slightest feeling of discomfort. His correct, conventional way of dressing, and his simple but self-assured manner, indicated his love of order and his inner serenity … At my first meeting with Freud I had the feeling of encountering a great personality (Gardiner, 1973: 155).

Pankejeff's reflections on his analysis with Freud can be found in Muriel Gardiner's edited collection, *The Wolf-Man and Sigmund Freud* (London: Pelican Books, 1973).

For introductions to hysteria, in Freud's work and beyond, see Julia Borossa's useful guide *Hysteria* (Cambridge: Icon Books, 2001), and Christopher Bollas's more sustained discussion, *Hysteria* (London: Routledge, 2000). For discussion of the role photography played in the 'invention' of hysteria, see Georges Didi-Huberman's *Invention of Hysteria: Charcot and the Photographic Iconography of the Salpêtrière*, translated by Alisa Hartz (Cambridge, MA: MIT Press, 2003).

Much has been written on the possible philosophical forebears of Freud's ideas. For Freud's connections with Schopenhauer, see Richard Bilsker, 'Freud and Schopenhauer: Consciousness, the Unconscious, and the Drive Towards Death', *Idealistic Studies*, 27, 1997, pp. 79–90; Jerry S. Clegg, 'Freud and the Issue of

Pessimism', *Schopenhauer Jahrbuch*, 61, 1980, pp. 37–50; Joshua Foa Dienstag, *Pessimism: Philosophy, Ethic, Spirit* (Princeton: Princeton University Press, 2006); and Christopher Young and Andrew Brook, 'Schopenhauer and Freud', *International Journal of Psychoanalysis*, 75, 1994, pp. 101–18. Schopenhauer's description of the mind comes from *The World as Will and Representation*, Vol. 2, trans. E.F.J. Payne (New York: Dover, 1844) 1966, p. 135.

On the connections with Nietzsche, see Ronald Lehrer, *Nietzsche's Presence in Freud's Life and Thought: On the Origins of a Psychology of Dynamic Unconscious Mental Functioning* (New York: State University of New York Press, 1995); Bruce Mazlish, 'Freud and Nietzsche', *Psychoanalytic Review*, 55 (3), 1968, pp. 360–75; and Paul Roazen, 'Nietzsche and Freud: Two Voices from the Underground', *Psychohistory Review*, 19 (3), 1991, pp. 327–48. Freud's claim that he 'did not know' Nietzsche is reported by Paul Federn in *Minutes of the Vienna Psycho-Analytic Society*, Vol. 11, 1906–8, pp. 355–61.

Freud's relationships with women are worth exploring because they go some way towards challenging the view of him as a chauvinistic patriarch whose ideas enshrine the notion that woman can be nothing but a mother, caught up in the reproductive drives of nature. For details both of the feminist critique and a response to it, see Juliet Mitchell, *Psychoanalysis and Feminism* (Harmondsworth: Penguin, 1975). Lisa Appignanesi and John Forrester's *Freud's Women* (London: Phoenix, 2005) provides detailed discussion of all the women in Freud's life, as well as offering a particularly interesting account of his relationship with Lou Andreas-Salomé. They also provide details of Andreas-Salomé's distinctive approach to psychoanalysis. The citations from Andreas-Salomé are from p. 243 and p. 268. For a glimpse into her thoughts on the relationship with Freud, see *The Freud Journal of Lou Andreas-Salomé*, translated and edited by Stanley A. Leavy (New York: Basic Books, 1964). For details of Marie Bonaparte's life and ideas and her relationship with Freud, see Célia Bertin's

Marie Bonaparte: A Life (New Haven: Yale University Press, 1982). For an account of the life of his wife, Martha Bernays, see Katja Behling's *Martha Freud* (Cambridge: Polity Press, 2005). For details of the feminist challenge to his focus on male relationships, and particularly the father–son relationship, see Christiane Olivier, *Jocasta's Children: The Imprint of the Mother* (London: Routledge, 1989); and Angela Carter, *The Sadeian Woman: An Exercise in Cultural History* (London: Virago, 1979). For Melanie Klein's reflections on the role of the mother and the breast, see 'Notes on Some Schizoid Mechanisms' in *Envy and Gratitude and Other Works 1946–1963* (London: Hogarth, 1975) pp. 1–24.

For details of Anna Freud's life and work, see Elisabeth Young-Bruehl, *Anna Freud: A Biography* (New York: WW Norton & Co, 1994). For her most important work, see *The Ego and the Mechanisms of Defence* (London: Hogarth Press, 1936). Freud's reflections on Anna's importance are from Gay's *Freud: A Life for Our Time*, p. 650.

For a concise account of Freud's different theories of the mind, see Richard Wollheim, *Freud* (London: Fontana, 1971). For a more developed discussion, see Joseph Sandler, Alex Holder, Christopher Dare and Anna Ursula Dreher, *Freud's Models of the Mind: An Introduction* (London: Karnac, 1997).

For those interested in finding out more about the different ways in which psychoanalysis has developed since Freud's death, see Stephen Mitchell and Margaret Black's *Freud and Beyond: A Modern History of Psychoanalytic Thought* (New York: Basic Books, 1995).

The transmission of Freud's ideas through popular culture, and particularly film, has been a source of interest to contemporary theorists of psychoanalysis. As well as explicitly informing the work of filmmakers, psychoanalytic theory has provided a way of reading films. For a useful collection of essays on psychoanalytic film criticism, see E. Ann Kaplan's *Psychoanalysis and Cinema* (London: Routledge, 1990). Nietzsche's claim that man may be the sickliest of all animals but definitely the most interesting comes from *The Anti-Christ* (1895) §14. Here, the translation is by R.J. Hollingdale (London: Penguin, 1990) p. 136.

Chapter 2

A good, short introduction to hysteria is to be found in Julia Borossa's *Hysteria* (Cambridge: Icon Books, 2001); her reflections on the hysteric not being listened to are to be found on p. 20. For details of Freud's cases that put them in a broader context, see Lisa Appignanesi and John Forrester, *Freud's Women*, (London: Phoenix, 2005) chapters 3 & 5; and Peter Gay's, *Freud: A Life for Our Time* (London: Macmillan, [1988]1995) pp. 69–87, 246–255.

The role of the case study may have caused Freud some disquiet but this is often the easiest way in to psychoanalytic ideas. For some contemporary case studies that are as fascinating as Freud's own, see Irving Yalom's *Love's Executioner and Other Tales of Psychotherapy* (London: Penguin, 1991), and most recently Stephen Grosz's *The Examined Life: How We Find and Lose Ourselves* (London: Chatto & Windus, 2013).

The diagnosis of hysteria is controversial and has formed the focus for critical feminist readings of psychoanalysis. Charles Bernheimer and Claire Kahane's edited collection *In Dora's Case: Freud, Hysteria, Feminism* (London: Virago, 1985) provides a good collection of essays that address this issue as well as Dora's case more broadly. Important contributions are Neil Hertz on 'Dora's Secrets, Freud's Techniques' (pp. 221–42) and Steven Marcus on 'Freud and Dora: Story, History, Case History' (pp. 56–91). For details of Dora's later friendship with Frau K, see Appignanesi and Forrester's *Freud's Women*, p. 167.

More recently, psychoanalysts have returned to hysteria to reassess its relevance as a diagnosis. See Christopher Bollas, *Hysteria* (London: Routledge, 2000) and Juliet Mitchell, *Mad Men and Medusas: Reclaiming Hysteria* (New York: Basic Books, 2000).

Bollas's claim that hysteria reveals 'trouble with the body' is to be found on p. 19 of his book.

If Freud identifies transference at work in the Dora case, it is left to later analysts to explore more fully the ways in which it might be used in psychoanalytic practice. This is particularly important in Kleinian psychoanalytic practice: see Melanie Klein's 'The Origins of Transference' in *Envy and Gratitude and Other Works 1946–1963* (London: Hogarth, [1952] 1975) pp. 48–56. For the clearest statement of the use of transference in Kleinian practice, see Betty Joseph's 'Transference: The Total Situation', *International Journal of Psychoanalysis*, 66, 1985, pp. 447–54. This is not to say, of course, that transference (and counter-transference) is not important for other schools of psychoanalysis. See for example, Donald Winnicott's 'On Transference', *International Journal of Psychoanalysis*, 37, 1956, pp. 386–8; and 'Hate in the Counter-transference' in his *Collected Papers: Through Pediatrics to Psychoanalysis* (New York: Basic Books, 1958), pp. 194–203. The latter provides a fine example of an analyst seeking to go where Freud did not. For a rather different perspective on this phenomenon – that of Lacanian analysis – see Jacques Lacan's 'Intervention on Transference' in Bernheimer and Kahane (1951), pp. 92–104.

On the later psychoanalytic understanding of the relationship between phantasy and reality, see Jean Laplanche and Jean-Bertrand Pontalis's 'Fantasy and the Origins of Sexuality', in Riccardo Steiner's edited collection *Unconscious Phantasy* (London: Karnac, 2003) pp. 107–14; and Hanna Segal's 'Phantasy and Reality', also in Steiner, pp. 199–209. Segal has also written on the relationship between creativity and phantasy in her 'Imagination, Play and Art', also in Steiner's collection, pp. 211–21.

Chapter 3

It is worth reading Sophocles' *Oedipus Rex* in *The Theban Plays* (E.F. Watling's translation for Penguin, 1947, is easily available) to identify the parts of the story foregrounded in Freud's theory, as well as the different ways in which it might be read. Note that in the play, Jocasta is a much more ambiguous figure than her portrayal as 'mother' in Freud's theory. To escape her fate (death at the hands of her child), Jocasta exposes Oedipus, leaving him to what she assumes will be his death.

Freud also draws on another much-performed play, Shakespeare's *Hamlet*, claiming that Hamlet's inability to avenge his father's death by killing his uncle Claudius, who has assumed the throne and married Gertrude, Hamlet's mother, can only be explained by the Oedipus complex. Hamlet cannot punish Claudius, because in Claudius's act he unconsciously recognizes his childhood desire to kill his father to attain exclusive possession of his mother (see Freud, 1897: 266; 1900: 265).

For feminists, the Oedipus complex, derived from male experience, has led to questions about the extent to which psychoanalysis can be of value to women. A good example of this feminist critique is in Toril Moi's essay, 'Representation of Patriarchy: Sexuality and Epistemology in Freud's Dora', *In Dora's Case: Freud, Feminism and Hysteria*, ed. C. Bernheimer and C. Kahane (London: Virago, 1985) pp. 181–199. French feminists such as Luce Irigaray, trained in Lacanian psychoanalysis, have focused on the idea of whether there is a distinctive female experience that is more than simply an identity defined in opposition to values supposedly held by the male. Lacan claims that there is no such thing as 'Woman', for the concept 'Woman' arises purely as a reverse projection of the values, language, and experience of masculinity (see Lacan's essay, 'God and the Jouissance of The Woman: A Love Letter', in *Feminine Sexuality: Jacques Lacan and the Ecole Freudienne*, eds Juliet Mitchell and Jacqueline Rose (Basingstoke: Macmillan, 1982) pp. 137–61. Irigaray's *This Sex Which Is Not One*, trans. C. Porter (Ithaca, NY: Cornell University Press, 1985) provides a response, suggesting ways of establishing a genuine female alterity (or 'otherness') that arises from female experience and is not dependent on male categorizing.

The claim that attaining genuine womanhood entails putting aside sexual pleasure located in the clitoris is most famously challenged in Anne Koedt's essay, 'The Myth of the Vaginal Orgasm' (in Sneja Gunew's edited collection, *A Reader in Feminist Knowledge*, London: Routledge, 1991, pp. 326–34). Another contentious issue surrounds the moral implications of the route Freud ascribes to the female version of the Oedipus complex. The conclusion that women are somehow less moral than men is limited neither to Freud nor to the world after psychoanalysis. For an example of a similar perspective, albeit philosophical rather than psychoanalytic, see Immanuel Kant's *Of the Beautiful and Sublime* (1764). For an early response to Freud that suggests a rather different way of reading this claim, see Lou Andreas-Salomé's *Zum Typus Weib* (Imago 3, 1914) pp. 1–14, in which she claims that women are much happier than men because they are not in thrall to the superego.

Many critics have focused their fire on the Oedipus complex. For a succinct account of their criticisms, see Michael Palmer's *Freud and Jung on Religion* (London: Routledge, 1997). For Malinowski's early criticisms of the complex, see *Sex and Repression in Savage Society* (London: RKP, 1927). That there are weaknesses in Freud's application of the Oedipus complex to his clinical work has been acknowledged by contemporary psychoanalysts. R.D. Hinshelwood's 'Little Hans's Transference' (*Journal of Child Psychotherapy*, 15, 1989, pp. 63–78) provides a good example of how Freud's interpretations seem to force clinical material to fit the pattern provided by his account of the Oedipus complex. For an example of an analysis that seems a little too concerned to replicate Freud's reading, see Ruth Mack Brunswick's 'A Supplement to Freud's "History of an Infantile Neurosis"' (1928) in Muriel Gardiner's edited collection *The Wolf Man and Sigmund Freud* (London: Hogarth Press, 1973).

The Oedipus complex remains a central feature of contemporary psychoanalytic theory, where it is read in ways that differ significantly from Freud's formulation. For Melanie Klein's object-relations reworking of the complex see her essays 'The Early Development of Conscience in the Child', (in *The Works of Melanie Klein*, London: Virago 1988 Vol. 2, 1933, pp. 248–57); and 'The Oedipus Complex in the Light of Early Anxieties' (in *The Writings of Melanie Klein*, London: Virage 1988 Vol. 1, 1945, pp. 370–419). Ronald Britton's 'The Missing Link: Parental Sexuality in the Oedipus Complex' (in John Steiner's edited collection *The Oedipus Complex Today*, London: Karnac, 1989) develops the Kleinian account by focusing on the importance of the child's recognition of their parents' relationship; a relationship that does not include him or her. A similar perspective is developed in the French psychoanalyst Julia Kristeva's description of the child's relationship with the mother. In 'Stabat Mater' (in *A Kristeva Reader*, ed. Toril Moi, New York: Columbia University Press, 1986, pp. 160–86) she uses her experience of motherhood to explore the separation from the symbiotic relationship with the mother that is necessary if relationship with others is to become a reality. That it might be possible to read the complex differently is also a feature of Juliet Mitchell's *Siblings* (Cambridge: Polity, 2003). Mitchell concentrates on the horizontal expression of the complex in the relationship between siblings, rather than the hierarchical account that dominates Freud's rendition.

For a fuller discussion of Freud on Eros and Thanatos, see my *Sex and Death* (Cambridge: Polity, 2002) Chapter 3. For Donald Winnicott's comments on the death instinct, see 'Creativity and Its Origins' in *Playing and Reality* (London: Routledge, 1971) pp. 87–114. For an account that takes the notion of the death-drive seriously and that relates it to later psychoanalytic theory, see Rob Weatherill's *The Sovereignty of Death* (London: Rebus Press, 1998). For Neville Symington's comments on the influence of

Brentano on Freud's attempt to develop a metapsychology, see his *The Blind Man Sees* (London: Karnac, 2004), Chapter 2.

What kind of practice is psychoanalysis? Bruno Bettelheim's *Freud and Man's Soul* (London: Hogarth Press, 1983) suggests a literary rendition of its key ideas, notably the Oedipus complex. Paul Ricoeur's *Freud and Philosophy: An Essay on Interpretation* (New Haven and London: Yale Press, 1970) suggests a similar perspective. Stephen Grosz's recent book, *The Examined Life* (London: Chatto & Windus, 2013) draws on the power of literature and story-telling for understanding psychoanalytic therapy. Interpretations of this kind, which focus on narrative, challenge Freud's attempt to anchor its practice and findings in empirical science (see Freud's 'The Scientific Project for Psychology', *SE 1*, ([1895] 1950) pp. 295–397). Many psychoanalysts would be far from happy with this move towards a narrative understanding of their discipline. An example of the attempt to anchor the practices and theories of psychoanalysis through applying the methods of empirical research can be found in Peter Fonagy's *Attachment Theory and Psychoanalysis* (New York: Other Press, 2001).

Some books have a peculiar ability to charm and irritate. For one such, see Camille Paglia's *Sexual Personae* (Harmondsworth: Penguin, 1991) which includes her comments on women and civilization.

Chapter 4

The different models that Freud applies as he investigates the processes of the mind are well described by Richard Wollheim in his *Freud* (1971). While Wollheim's approach to Freud is principally philosophical, Joseph Sandler, Alex Holder, Christopher Dare and Anna Ursula Dreher offer a specifically psychoanalytic rendition of these stages in his thought in their *Freud's Models of the Mind: An Introduction* (London: Karnac, 1997).

The issue of how to read Freud and the role of Strachey's English translation in shaping the image of Freud as a developmental psychologist remains live. For discussion of the English translation of Freud, see Riccardo Steiner's 'To Explain Our Point of View to English Readers in English Words', *International Review of Psychoanalysis*, 18, 1991, pp. 351–92. It is worth noting that Freud thoroughly approved of the systematizing of psychoanalysis that Steiner identifies, feeling that it aligned his nascent discipline more closely with the natural sciences. See 'Some Elementary Lessons in Psychoanalysis' (1940) for Freud's comments on this process.

The reading of Freud promoted by Lacan is explained well in the first chapter of Joël Dor's *Introduction to the Reading of Lacan* (New York: Other Press, 1998). The emphasis on Freud's earlier writings, which shapes Lacanian analysis, continues to be significant, not just in France but increasingly in Anglophone psychoanalysis. For an example of what this might mean for reading Freud, see Rosine Perelberg's edited collection *Freud: A Modern Reader* (London: Whurr, 2005).

The psychoanalytic construction of time and how it relates to the different psychic agencies is of great importance for French psychoanalysis. See André Green's identification of the two experiences of time in his *Time in Psychoanalysis: Some Contradictory Aspects*, trans. A. Weller (London: Free Association Books, 2002) and his article 'The Construction of Heterochrony' in *Time and Memory* ed. Rosine Perelberg (London: Karnac, 2007) pp. 1–22 for detailed examination of this phenomenon. Perelberg's comment on the experience of time is from an unpublished paper, "Après Coup and Unconscious Phantasy". For further discussion of the significance of time for the French tradition in psychoanalysis, see Julia Kristeva's *Time and Sense* (New York: Columbia University Press, 1996).

Dream interpretation continues to lie at the heart of psychoanalytic practice. For contemporary discussions of the interpretation of dreams, see Sara Flanders, *The Dream Discourse Today* (London: Karnac, 1993). For the afterlife of the Irma dream, particularly as it relates to Freud's relationship with Fliess, see Peter Gay, *Freud: A Life for Our Times* (Basingstoke: Macmillan, 1989) pp. 84–7, 274–7. For a psychoanalytic account of the prophetic function of dreams, see Rosine Perelberg's 'The "Oracle" in Dreams: The Past and the Future in the Present' in her edited collection, *Dreaming and Thinking* (London: Karnac, 2000), pp. 109–28. For Julia Kristeva's claim that we are 'strangers to ourselves', see her book of that title, published by Columbia University Press, 1991.

For the Wolf Man's analysis with both Freud and Brunswick, see Muriel Gardner's *The Wolf Man and Sigmund Freud* (London: Pelican Books, 1973). For the Wolf Man's dream while in analysis with Brunswick, see Gardner p. 315. Rosine Perelberg's comments on the phenomenon of *après-coup*, cited here, come from her essay 'Unconscious Phantasy and Après-coup: "From the History of an Infantile Neurosis" (the Wolf Man)' in her edited collection *Freud: A Modern Reader*, pp. 206–23.

Recognizing the role of the timeless unconscious and the challenge that this makes to the notion of cure is best detailed in Freud's paper 'Analysis Terminable and Interminable' (*SE 23*, pp. 209–53). This raises the limits of psychoanalytic therapy and suggests some of the reasons for thinking of analysis as a means of developing character, an approach outlined by Wilhelm Reich in 'On Character Analysis' (1928) in R. Fliess's edited collection, *The Psychoanalytic Reader*, (New York, 1948: IUP), p. 106–23.

For an autobiography that captures perfectly the complex experience of time that shapes Freud's thinking, see Arthur Miller's *Timebends* (London: Methuen, 1987). As is often the case, a literary rendition is much clearer than many academic treatises on this phenomenon. The description given here of the child's view of the world is on p. 11.

Chapter 5

The perspective that Freud's writings of religion can only ever be read negatively is the one held by most commentators. A similarly common view is that his criticisms of religion are not particularly convincing. Critical readings of Freud's account of religion are plentiful. Peter Clarke and Peter Byrne give a handy synopsis of these criticisms in their *Religion Defined and Explained* (Basingstoke: Macmillan, 1993), pp. 200–2. For John Hick's comments, referred to in this chapter, see his *Philosophy of Religion* (Englewood Cliffs, NJ: Prentice-Hall, 1963), p. 36. Jonathan Lear's dismissive comments on Freud's relevance on religion are in his *Freud* (London: Routledge, 2005), p. 218.

   This is not to say that alternative voices have not been heard. James DiCenso's *The Other Freud* (London: Routledge, 1999) suggests that Freud's writings on religion are richer and more multi-faceted than his critics allow. DiCenso's perspective is informed by the ideas of the French psychoanalysts Jacques Lacan and Julia Kristeva and his approach connects post-modern thought with cultural theory and religious studies. Psychoanalytic perspectives are also subtly changing, revealing more in Freud's writings on this subject than might at first appear to be the case. Jonathan Lear's view in his *Freud* (London: Routledge, 2005), Chapter 7, that Freud's ideas have not stood the test of time and are far from useful, has been challenged by others who have sought a reappraisal of this aspect of his writings. Donald Capps, in his collection *Freud and the Freudians on Religion* (London: Yale University Press, 2001), argues for a more complex reading of Freud's theory of religion by considering the development of his ideas by later psychoanalysts. Mary Kay O'Neil and Salman Akhtar's collection of essays *On Freud's 'The Future of an Illusion'* (London: Karnac, 2009) similarly brings together atheists and those more sympathetic to religion to discuss different ways in which Freud might be read. In his introduction, Akhtar suggests

Freud's atheism is not as clear cut as we might, at first, imagine. A similar view is held by Alistair Ross, Director of Psychodynamic Studies and Dean of Kellogg College, Oxford. Ross argues that Freud's letters to his friend, the Swiss pastor Pfister, reveal a more sympathetic attitude to religious belief than might be derived from limiting one's reading to his published works on the subject. For this correspondence see Heinrich Meng and Ernst Freud's edited collection, *The Letters of Sigmund Freud and Oskar Pfister* (London: Hogarth Press, 1963). It might also be noted that Freud's theory of religion as a form of anthropomorphic projection has been used more recently by Stewart Guthrie in his attempt to develop a new theory of religion. Guthrie argues in his *Faces in the Clouds* (Oxford: OUP, 1993) that religion arises from the attempt to see the world as human-like. Rather than reject this as simply fallacious, Guthrie argues that it reveals much about the human fears that make it necessary to find psychic strategies that help render the world a safer place.

Michael Palmer's *Freud and Jung on Religion* (London: Routledge, 1997) offers an excellent account of the variety to be found in Freud's account of religion. A particularly interesting section is where Palmer draws attention to Freud's own superstitious tendencies, including discussion of the incident of the Broken Venus (pp. 10–12). Whether there are similarities between religion and superstition continues to be a topic for discussion in contemporary philosophy of religion. See for example the discussion between D.Z. Phillips and Terrence Tilley in *Journal of the American Academy of Religion*, 68 (2), 2000. For Phillips, 'genuine religion' is something quite distinct from superstition, and he highlights the difference between the religious attempt to align one's will to the will of God and the superstitious desire to change the mind of God. Tilley resists this view, arguing that to recognize the similarities between both perspectives need not lead to the rejection of religion but to the acknowledgement of the desire to connect with a wider world common to both ways of thinking and acting.

The translation of *Seelenleben* as 'inner life' is used by Nicola Luckhurst in her 2004 translation of *Studies in Hysteria* for Penguin. For Bettelheim's rendition of this as 'the life of the soul', see his *Freud and Man's Soul* (London: Hogarth Press, 1983).

Freud's use of the term 'fate' connects him once again to that figure whose writings he tried to ignore: Nietzsche. Nietzsche's idea of 'eternal recurrence' promotes the practice of *amor fati* ('the love of fate') rather more positively than Freud's account of how to accept fate. Eternal recurrence comprises the idea of how would we respond if we were told that we had to repeat our lives, in absolutely the same way, over and over, until the end of recorded time. Would we be delighted, or horrified? For Nietzsche, the aim is to not just to 'accept' fate but to *will* not just the good but also the bad in our lives. Only then can we really be said to love our fate. For Nietzsche's description of eternal recurrence see his *The Gay Science*, (1887) §341. For fuller discussion of this aspect of Nietzsche's thought, see Lawrence Hatab, *Nietzsche's Life Sentence: Coming to Terms with Eternal Recurrence* (London: Routledge, 2005).

The influence of philosophy on Freud's early years is detailed in William McGrath's *Freud's Discovery of Psychoanalysis* (Ithaca: Cornell, 1986), McGrath draws particular attention to his reading of Feuerbach while a medical student (pp. 101–7).

In considering Freud's different uses of fate, it is worth noting the distinction between fate and destiny offered by Christopher Bollas in *Forces of Destiny: Psychoanalysis and Human Idiom* (London: Free Association, 1989). Bollas defines fate as something outside the self that is largely understood negatively and passively, while destiny is that which can be seized and shaped as one's own. The relationship between destiny and character formation connects to the later stage of Freud's career where the focus shifts from understanding the unconscious to the work of character analysis. For discussion of what this involves, see Richard Sterba's 'The Fate of the Ego in Analytic Therapy', *International Journal of Psychoanalysis*, 15, 1934, pp. 117–26.

On the connections between religion and the uncanny, see Diane Jonte-Pace, *Speaking the Unspeakable: Religion, Misogyny and the Uncanny Mother in Freud's Cultural Texts* (Berkeley: University of California Press, 2001).

That Freud's ideas should resonate with aspects of Stoic thinking is hardly surprising: see R.H. Armstrong's *A Compulsion for Antiquity: Freud and the Ancient World* (Ithaca and London: Cornell University Press, 2005) for details of Freud's fascination with the ancient world. Peter Gay's *Freud: A Life for Our Time* (Basingstoke: Papermac, 1995) offers examples of the stoicism Freud showed when dealing with the blows of life. Of course, there is some difference between using this term loosely and adopting its belief structure as a framework for one's life. Having said that, it is worth reading the sections that deal with Freud's response to the death of his beloved daughter Sophie (pp. 391–3) and Gay's description of Freud's approach to his own death, which hint at the kind of antique disposition associated with the Stoic practice of the philosophers Seneca and Marcus Aurelius. Having suffered for many years with cancer of the jaw, Freud took charge of his own death as the pain became excruciating. At his request, his doctor, Max Schur, administered a fatal dose of morphine:

> Schur was on the point of tears as he witnessed Freud facing death with dignity and without self-pity. He had never seen anyone die like that … Nearly four decades earlier, Freud had written to Oskar Pfister wondering what one would do some day, 'when thoughts fail or words will not come'?

He could not suppress:

> 'A tremor before this possibility. That is why, with all the resignation before destiny that suits an honest man, I have one secret entreaty: only no invalidism, no paralysis of one's powers through bodily misery. Let us die in harness, as King

Macbeth says. He had seen to it that his secret entreaty would be fulfilled. The old stoic had kept control of his life to the end' (Gay, 1995: 651).

That Freud's therapeutic practice might have as its goal the fostering of the same kind of resilience and fortitude is therefore not surprising. That ancient philosophy might itself function as a form of therapy for life's ills is a position adopted in Pierre Hadot's *Philosophy as a Way of Life* (Oxford: Blackwell, 1995) and Martha Nussbaum's *The Therapy of Desire: Theory and Practice in Hellenistic Ethics* (Princeton: Princeton University Press, 1994).

For an article that runs only to three pages, 'On Transience' has elicited some creative and detailed responses. The most sustained engagement is Matthew von Unwerth's *Freud's Requiem* (London: Continuum, 2005). von Unwerth identifies Freud's companions as Rainer Maria Rilke and Lou Andreas-Salomé. Jonathan Dollimore, in *Death, Desire and Loss in Western Culture* (London: Penguin, 1998) does not take seriously Freud's argument for a third way between religious optimism and atheistic pessimism, arguing that this is a 'trite' response; a 'mischievous' intervention to an overly serious young man (p. 181). I disagree: Freud's approach opens up a different perspective and might profitably be pursued by the philosopher of religion: something I attempt in my *Sex and Death: A Reappraisal of Human Mortality* (Cambridge: Polity, 2002).

Chapter 6

The different possible readings of Freud make him a fascinating figure. For a recent collection of essays that present different readings of Freud from both British and French psychoanalysts, see Rosine Jozef Perelberg's edited collection *Freud: A Modern Reader* (London: Whurr, 2005). For an introduction to the kind of neuro-psychoanalysis that informs Mark Solms's adoption of

Freud for neuroscience, see his book, written with Oliver Turnbull, *The Brain and the Inner World: An Introduction to the Neuroscience of Subjective Experience* (London: Karnac, 2002). For William R. Uttal's critique of neuroscience, see his *The New Phrenology: The Limits of Localising Cognitive Processes in the Brain* (Cambridge, MA: MIT Press, 2001).

If you haven't read Vladimir Nabokov's *Lolita* (London: Penguin, [1955] 1980), you should. Highly controversial it may be; it is also funny, sensual, and surprising. Ultimately disturbing, its narrative form plays with the reader's response, inevitably casting the reader in the role of voyeur. For the passage cited here, see p. 282. At the same time, Nabokov's novel offers, I think, a more complex account of sexual abuse than is often the case. It is an account of the complex web that supports abusive sexual relationships, which resonates with recent criminal cases on child sex trafficking in the UK. In 2012, nine men from Rochdale were convicted of sexual offences against young girls who thought of these men as their boyfriends. In the context of a supposed relationship, these girls were handed over to others to abuse. To talk of these girls 'choosing' to take part in such acts makes little sense and the complexity of Freud's account of sexuality offers, I think, a better context for discussing the nature of such abuse than the dominant liberal language of choice and consent.

Much has been written about Freud's interest with and connections to philosophy. Bruno Bettelheim's *Freud and Man's Soul* (London: Hogarth Press, 1983) is a classic account, which frames Freud less as a scientist and more as a thinker who draws upon the humanities for understanding what Bettelheim calls 'our common humanity'. Freud's early philosophical interests are also explored in William J. McGrath's *Freud's Discovery of Psychoanalysis* (London: Cornell University Press, 1986), Chapter 3. McGrath suggesting that far from being irrelevant to the development of his ideas, philosophy played a crucial role. A similarly detailed exposition of Freud's philosophical connections is presented by

Alfred Tauber in his *Freud: The Reluctant Philosopher* (Princeton: Princeton University Press, 2010). For Joshua Foa Dienstag's fascinating discussion of Freud's metaphysical pessimism and its relationship to the philosophy of Arthur Schopenhauer, see his *Pessimism: Philosophy, Ethic, Spirit* (Princeton: Princeton University Press, 2006). For an insight into Freud's attitude to life and death, see Matthew von Unwerth's *Freud's Requiem: Mourning, Memory and the Invisible History of a Summer Walk* (London: Continuum, 2005). For details of the conversation with Marie Bonaparte detailed here, see p. 177. For the painful nature of Freud's death see Gay 1995, p. 651.

The claim that Freud's ideas might be relevant to critiquing the happiness agenda that continues to inform public policy connects the themes of cultural criticism and moral philosophy explored in this chapter. For one of the key texts that has informed such policy initiatives, see Richard Layard, *Happiness: Lessons from a New Science* (Harmondsworth: Penguin, 2005). For a collection of (often critical) essays on the current cultural obsession with promoting happiness and well-being, see John Atherton, Elaine Graham and Ian Steedman's edited collection *The Practices of Happiness* (London: Routledge, 2011).

Bibliography

Breuer, Josef and Sigmund Freud (1893–95), *Studies in Hysteria*, *Standard Edition of the Complete Works of Sigmund Freud*, Volume 2, translated and edited by J. Strachey, London: Hogarth Press/Virago

Freud, Ernst L., ed. (1960), *Letters of Sigmund Freud*, tr. T and J. Stern, New York: Basic Books

Freud, Sigmund ([1895] 1950), 'The Scientific Project for Psychology', *Standard Edition of the Complete Works of Sigmund Freud* (hereafter 'SE'), Volume 1, translated and edited by J. Strachey, London: Hogarth Press/Virago, pp. 295–397

Freud, Sigmund (1896), 'The Aetiology of Hysteria', SE 3, pp. 189–221

Freud, Sigmund (1897), 'Letter 71 to Fliess', SE 1, pp. 263–266

Freud, Sigmund (1899), 'Screen Memories', SE 3, pp. 299–322

Freud, Sigmund (1900), *The Interpretation of Dreams*, SE 4 & 5

Freud, Sigmund (1901), *The Psychopathology of Everyday Life*, SE 6

Freud, Sigmund (1905a [1901]), 'Fragment of an Analysis of a Case of Hysteria', SE 7, pp. 7–122

Freud, Sigmund (1905b), 'Three Essays on the Theory of Sexuality', SE 7, pp. 135–243

Freud, Sigmund (1905c), *Jokes and Their Relation to the Unconscious*, SE 8

Freud, Sigmund (1907), 'Obsessive Actions and Religious Practices,' SE 9, pp. 115–127

Freud, Sigmund (1908a [1907]), 'Creative Writers and Day-Dreaming', SE 9, pp. 141–153

Freud, Sigmund (1908b), 'On the Sexual Theories of Children,' SE 9, pp. 209–226

Freud, Sigmund (1909a), 'Analysis of a Phobia in a Five-Year-Old Boy', SE 10, pp. 5–149

Freud, Sigmund (1909b), 'Notes Upon a Case of Obsessional Neurosis', SE 10, pp. 155–318

Freud, Sigmund (1911), 'Formulations on the Two Principles of Mental Functioning', SE 12, pp. 213–226.

Freud, Sigmund (1912), 'The Dynamics of Transference', SE 12, pp. 97–108

Freud, Sigmund (1913a), 'Totem and Taboo', SE 13, pp. 1–162

Freud, Sigmund (1913b), 'The Claims of Psychoanalysis to Scientific Interest', SE 13, pp. 165–190

Freud, Sigmund (1914a), 'Remembering, Repeating and Working Through,' SE 12, pp. 145–156

Freud, Sigmund (1914b), 'On the History of the Psycho-Analytic Movement', SE 14, pp. 1–66

Freud, Sigmund (1914c), 'The Moses of Michelangelo', SE 13, pp. 211–238

Freud, Sigmund (1915a [1914]), 'Observations on Transference-Love', SE 12, pp. 157–171

Freud, Sigmund (1915b), 'Instincts and Their Vicissitudes', SE 14, pp. 109–140

Freud, Sigmund (1916 [1915]), 'On Transience', SE 14, pp. 303–307

Freud, Sigmund (1916–1917), *Introductory Lectures on Psycho-Analysis*, SE 15 & 16

Freud, Sigmund ([1915] 1917), 'Mourning and Melancholia', SE 14, pp. 237–258

Freud, Sigmund ([1914] 1918), 'From the History of an Infantile Neurosis', SE 17, pp. 3–122

Freud, Sigmund (1919), 'The 'Uncanny'', SE 17: 217–256

Freud, Sigmund (1920), 'Beyond the Pleasure Principle', SE 18, pp. 1–64

Freud, Sigmund (1923a), 'The Ego and the Id', SE 19, pp. 3–66

Freud, Sigmund (1923b), 'The Infantile Genital Organization', SE 19, pp. 141–145

Freud, Sigmund (1924a), 'The Economic Problem of Masochism', SE 19, pp. 155–170

Freud, Sigmund (1924b), 'The Dissolution of the Oedipus Complex', SE 19, pp. 171–179

Freud, Sigmund (1925a), 'An Autobiographical Study', SE 20, pp. 1–74

Freud, Sigmund (1925b), 'Some Psychical Consequences of the Anatomical Distinction between the Sexes', SE 19, pp. 248–258

Freud, Sigmund (1927a), 'The Future of an Illusion', SE 21, pp. 1–56.

Freud, Sigmund (1927b), 'Fetishism', SE 21, pp. 147–157

Freud, Sigmund (1928 [1927]), 'Dostoyevsky and Parricide', SE 21, pp. 173–196

Freud, Sigmund (1930 [1929]), 'Civilisation and Its Discontents', SE 21, pp. 57–145

Freud, Sigmund (1931), 'Female Sexuality', SE 21, pp. 221–243

Freud, Sigmund ([1932] 1933), 'New Introductory Lectures on Psycho-Analysis', SE 22, pp. 5–182

Freud, Sigmund (1936), 'A Disturbance of Memory on the Acropolis', SE 22, 237–248

Freud, Sigmund (1937a), 'Analysis Terminable and Interminable', SE 23, pp. 209–253.

Freud, Sigmund (1937b), 'Constructions in Analysis', SE 23, pp. 255–269

Freud, Sigmund (1939), 'Moses and Monotheism', SE 23, pp. 3–137

Freud, Sigmund ([1938]1940), 'An Outline of Psychoanalysis', SE 23, pp. 141–207

Freud, Sigmund and Josef Breuer (2004), *Studies in Hysteria*, translated by N. Luckhurst, London: Penguin

Meng, Heinrich and Ernst Freud, eds. (1963), *The Letters of Sigmund Freud and Oskar Pfister*, tr. Eric Mosbacher, London: Hogarth Press

Acknowledgements

This book took shape over a number of years, and I would like to thank the following for their insights and support during its writing:

Colleagues at Oxford Brookes University, especially Dominic Corrywright, Tom Cosgrove, Martin Groves, Perry Hinton, Michele Paule, Constantine Sandis, and Tom Tyler.

The Psychoanalysis Unit at University College London, who provided numerous insights and new ways of seeing over the course of my Masters studies there. Special thanks go to Lionel Bailly, Michael Brearley, Nicola Luckhurst, Ruth McCall, and Rosine Perelberg.

Colleagues involved in the Philosophy, Theology and the Therapeutic Group, especially Madelyn Brewer, John Cottingham, Penny Hill, Liana New, and Michael Parsons.

Alistair Ross, who was a careful and thoughtful reader of the manuscript.

Mike Harpley at Oneworld for his thoughts and comments and Ann Grand for her painstaking reading of the text and for keeping my sentences in order.

My brother Brian R. Clack, for the many illuminating discussions of Freud's work that we have had and continue to have.

And most of all my husband, Robert Lindsey, for bringing his incisive mind to bear on the sometimes rambling and disconnected thoughts that I had during the writing of this book and for showing me, in ways of which Freud would no doubt approve, that life involves not just work but love too.

Index